"The Christian life is not about a mom... It is about a lifetime of faith that endu... ...Ritchie has written a helpful guide on how to cultivate faith that will endure until the end of our days."

DAYTON HARTMAN
lead pastor, Redeemer Church (Rocky Mount, North Carolina);
author of *Jesus Wins* and *Church History for Modern Ministry*

"If anyone can speak to the nature of Christian endurance, it is Daniel Ritchie, whose courageous life is both an inspiration and a witness to the power of the gospel. With clarity and compassion, Ritchie spills out biblical truth, born not from academic musings but from the grit of everyday life. If you are in the midst of despair, if you are struggling to make sense of your life, if you are weighed down with burdens that seem too hard to carry, this book will point you to the one who promises to make your yoke light. Read this book and find Jesus on every page.

DANIEL DARLING
contributor to USA Today;
author of *A Way With Words* and *The Dignity Revolution*

"Daniel's book is as powerful and insightful as his testimony. I can assure you that you've never met another Christian like Daniel, and his book will impact you at a fundamental level. God has written his story in a way that enables him to speak with authority on building a faith that lasts."

J.D. GREEAR
pastor, The Summit Church (Raleigh-Durham);
author of *Just Ask!*

"Hebrews 12:1–3 teaches us that when God saves us He calls us to run a long-distance race with endurance. It is one thing to begin this race well, but it is another thing to finish it well. My friend Daniel Ritchie has provided us a biblically and experientially rich road map to run well and finish well with our eyes glued to Jesus. This is a book that will bless and encourage many."

DANIEL L. AKIN
president, Southeastern Baptist Theological Seminary

"The call to faithfully endure in the midst of trials and hard times in life is a recurring theme in Scripture. Learning how to endure is helpful. Knowing someone who is actually an example of what it means to endure is better. This is why I believe so much in Daniel Ritchie and his book, Endure: Building Faith for the Long Run. For Daniel, endurance is not just some theoretical or theological concept. It's been his life. He has his doctorate in the school of difficulty and has handled it with grace and joy. If you want a practical guide to getting through tough times, written by someone who knows what he is talking about, this book is for you. Read it and you will be inspired, encouraged, and challenged to keep running your race, no matter what you may be up against."

JARRETT STEPHENS
pastor of Champion Forest Baptist Church, Houston, Texas;
author of *The Always God: He Hasn't Changed* and *You Are Not Forgotten*

"Faith is not a sentimental leap into the unknown. It is a gift from God given for our perseverance in him. This is why I'm thankful for Daniel Ritchie's Endure. This book is designed to help you in every stage of your journey with God—through discouragement, doubt, and suffering. This is the stuff our faith is made for, and this is the stuff Endure will equip you to press through by God's grace."

JARED C. WILSON
assistant professor of pastoral ministry at Midwestern Seminary;
author of *Love Me Anyway*

"It is easy to 'flame out.' I mean, we see it all the time--ministers disqualifying themselves or running ragged until they burn out. But it does not have to be that way. In Endure, Daniel Ritchie will help you rekindle that flame to keep moving forward in life and in ministry. I especially appreciated how very well he saturated it with Scripture from beginning to end. Buy this book, read this book, and I believe it will help you go a long way in enduring through the end to the glory of God."

MATT HENSLEE
associational mission strategist, Collin Baptist Association;
author of *Jonah Over Coffee*

BUILDING FAITH

ENDURE

FOR THE
LONG RUN

BUILDING FAITH

ENDURE

FOR THE

LONG RUN

DANIEL RITCHIE

KIRKDALE PRESS

Endure: Building Faith for the Long Run

Copyright 2022 Daniel Ritchie

Kirkdale Press, an imprint of Lexham Press
1313 Commercial St., Bellingham, WA 98225
LexhamPress.com

Print ISBN 9781683595410
Digital ISBN 9781683595427
Library of Congress Control Number 2021941979

Lexham Editorial: Allisyn Ma, Abigail Stocker, Kelsey Matthews
Cover Design: Joshua Hunt, Brittany Schrock
Typesetting: Justin Marr

TEAGUE AND ELLIOTT—

HE IS WITH YOU ALWAYS.
NEVER STOP CHASING HIM.

CONTENTS

INTRODUCTION

T here are two things in life you never pray for: brokenness and patience.

Obviously that's a joke. It's a joke you will hear pastors offer up in light of the weight that both prayers carry when it comes to living them out. A prayer for brokenness is a call for loss and affliction. Being broken tears away any sort of veneer of self-sufficiency by having to walk through hurt and darkness.

A prayer for patience functions much in the same way as a prayer for brokenness. The answered prayer for patience does not come with an immediate snap of the fingers. The prayer for patience is answered in the opportunities to be patient. If patience were a muscle, these opportunities give the muscle a workout—and, as we see with physical fitness, patience isn't built in a day. Time is a necessary part of our growth as both a person and as a child of God.

Yet the wait is the worst part of one's growth in patience. The wait is filled with questions and doubts that haunt our waking hours. Especially when the wait is partnered with pain, our questions loom large. Our prayers sound a lot like, "God, what are you doing?" or even, "God, why me? Why aren't you getting me out of this painful wait?"

The problem with patience is that the most human reaction we have is to look for an immediate remedy to our problems or for the endgame of our growth. We want answers right now and on our terms, which is not the typical way God works. He works in the lives of His children over the long run, not just in the immediate circumstances.

Paul met Jesus on the road to Damascus but was quickly met with doubters and detractors, which pushed him into anonymity for nearly three years. Abraham went, and then he waited. Joseph saw more than a decade pass between the betrayal by his brothers and his eventual ascension to overseer to the king of Egypt.

Each situation saw a lot of waiting and a lot of silence—but that did not mean God was absent. His plan was on the move, and His fingerprints were evident in each waiting period. There was pain and betrayal. Each man slammed up against insecurity and doubt. The days crept by as they waited for what was next. But even in the wait, they didn't stop and didn't quit.

As they waited, God was working. He was molding and shaping them for what was to come in their lives, even years into the future. God's purposes were operating on a timeline that none of these men had any concept of. God was—and still is—One who is not constrained by the tyranny of the immediate. He was growing these men in their faith while also using them as instruments of His glory.

These days, God is no different in how He works and moves among those who trust Him. He still works in the miraculous and the immediate, and He also takes His time in growing the faith of the children He loves so dearly. His work in our lives is aimed at growing us into Christlikeness every day, not in an instant at conversion.

So what do we do with the wait, with the work, with the relationships, and with the ministry opportunities that lay before us?

That is what we will look at over the course of this book. Through every aspect of our lives, what can we do to grow in Christ while showing the world more of Christ? No matter what season of life we are in—plenty or hunger, abundance or need, wait or work—we can still be about our Father's purposes. We know that "he who began a good work in you will bring it to completion at the day of Jesus Christ" (Philippians 1:6).

Until that day, we will live and trust God, knowing that there are rhythms to sow into our lives right now that will help us grow in Christ while also bringing glory to the One we love.

It is time to learn to endure.

CHAPTER 1

WHY IT'S HARD TO ENDURE

Look carefully then how you walk, not as unwise but as wise,
making the best use of the time, because the days are evil.
EPHESIANS 5:15-16

I accepted Jesus as Lord for myself as a fifteen-year-old, and it certainly was the moment that changed my life. At the time, I was a hope-starved teen defining his worth by the opinions of others. That is a death trap of identity and worth unto itself, but there were several factors that deepened my self-loathing and insecurity.

I was born without arms, and I've spent my entire life living in a world meant for hands without having the benefit of them. Everything I learned to do in my formative years was an uphill battle of trial and error. I had to learn to do everyday tasks—eating, writing, dressing myself, opening doors, typing on a computer, driving a car—by watching how others accomplished those tasks with their hands and then figuring out how to adapt those actions for my toes. While there were several victories throughout these formative years, I was marked by consistent failure.

As I tried my best to adapt to my surroundings, something odd started to happen in my heart. I would watch people write or eat and I couldn't help but notice how easily they used their hands in comparison to how I used my clunky feet. Everyone else had the one thing I wanted. It was the one thing I would never have. Arms.

All this personal strife weighed heavily on me but so did the pressure from the outside. Being different than nearly every other person on the planet made me a target for the stares and rude comments of those whom I met on a daily basis. A simple trip to the grocery store guaranteed people would stare at me. In part, I knew people were genuinely curious about what they were seeing unfold in front of them, but there was also a heaviness that came with being watched everywhere I went.

Then there were the comments from other people. The unprompted, unexpected, unkind comments: Gross, Freak, Weirdo, Cripple, Circus Act. Even now those words linger in the back of my mind, and as much as they hurt now, those words landed even harder when I was a kid. They left me with the inescapable feeling of being attacked and unloved. The outside world recognized that I was different and had little issue with letting me know.

I felt like I was under siege from all sides. My hurt and insecurity were in fresh supply from both my inner man and from the outside world. This dark time stretched on for much of my teenage years, but it finally reached a peak when I was fifteen. I had totally isolated myself because of my self-contempt but also because of my disdain for others. I was bitter, frustrated, angry, lonely, and depressed.

Yet in this time of darkness and despair, God showed me His love for me as revealed in the gospel. I saw His pursuit of my wayward life. I saw His power displayed in loosening the chains of sin and death through His Son's death and resurrection on the cross. The light of His gospel was shining into my darkness and putting everything into clear view: my sin, my hurt, my selfishness, His grace, His love, and His glory.

On a cold March morning in 1999, I confessed and abided in Jesus as my Lord, and from that moment things began to change in my heart and my life. My language of self-loathing morphed into a recognition of the fearfully and wonderfully wrought life that God had made. My cold heart toward others began to thaw with an innate love that I had never experienced before. Things in my life were beginning to change, but they were changing very slowly.

The speed of the change is what surprised me more than anything. I expected to pray a prayer and then—poof!—everything about my life would be perfect. There would be no more doubt, no more insecurity, and no more trials. I thought Jesus was going to make everything better and do that instantly.

Oddly enough, that was not something that was ever taught to me by my parents or any pastor that I had ever come across. It was the expectation of my impatient heart. My thought was that if I had this new life in Christ (Colossians 3:4), then it would be something that happened all at once, but that is not what happened at all.

Failure was still a very present part of my life, but so was my strong God. In my early days in Christ, I gripped tightly to the promise that I could do all things through Christ who gives me strength (Philippians 4:13). I was still prone to loathe myself and my armlessness, but I also knew there was not anything in all of creation that could separate me from the love of God (Romans 8:39). There were still people who stared at and criticized me, but there was also the voice of Christ speaking over my life: "Come to me, all who labor and are heavy laden, and I will give you rest" (Matthew 11:28).

My life had changed in incredible ways, but not at the speed I had initially anticipated. The circumstances that triggered my inner wounds were still the same, but I now had a way of navigating it all with hope. There was no instantaneous fix to the issues of my life, but there was an instant Advocate and Lord with me through it all. My initial assumptions about the speed at which God was going to change my brokenness were totally wrong, but that did not mean He was distant from me. It only meant that He was at work in my life by His means and His timeline. And that is a good thing.

Even today, God is clearly at work in my life according to His timing and His kindness. Yet, I still think back on those early assumptions that I had about God and the speed at which I thought He would bring about Christlike fruit in my life. How did I come to the place where I thought that sanctifying change would occur at the speed of light?

I was groomed by the world to think that way.

By the time I came to rest in Jesus as Savior and Lord, it was the late '90s, and the pulse of the culture at large was quickening on every conceivable level. Growing up, my dad traveled for his job, and dinners were often just my mom and me. To save a little work and time for my mom, we would have a microwave dinner at least once a week. Pop a tray in the microwave for three minutes and *voilà*—dinner!

My teenage years saw the entrance of the Internet into people's homes. If you needed an answer to a question, all you had to do was plug your computer into your home's phone line and you were connected to the World Wide Web. Never again would I have to scan the pages of an encyclopedia to find answers for my homework. All I needed was Yahoo.

I remember my parents getting their first cell phone when I was in elementary school. It was a clunky, gray Motorola flip phone. It didn't have the best cell signal, and the battery life was incredibly short, but it allowed you to reach family members and friends in ways that were impossible before. Gone were the days where we had to hunt down a pay phone to make a phone call. Now my mom had a phone in her purse.

The world seemed like a smaller place, with every technological advance pushing the culture forward. That was more than twenty years ago now, and little did I realize that it was just a glimpse of the gains that were to come over the next two decades. Connection, accessibility, and the exchange of ideas were about to hit hyper-speed.

The dawn of the new millennium was the start of so much newness for me. I welcomed in the year 2000 by preaching for my very first time at a youth group event to over 250 students. I had no idea what I was doing, and I had no idea that preaching would be the call of my life.

I had several amazing conversations that night following the youth group lock-in. Oddly enough, through the course of these conversations, at least three students mentioned a website called Myspace. I had no idea what this website was all about, but I signed up for a profile the next day. Little did I know the massive cultural footprint that social media was about to leave.

Later in 2000, I finally got a cell phone for the first time. I had just started driving (yes, I drive with my feet), and my parents felt like it was a good idea to get me a cell phone in case I ever broke down or needed them while I was out of town. I struggled to push the tiny buttons with my plump toes, but I was determined to figure it out. That little flip phone was the first of many cell phones that led to me having the footheld computer that I have today in my iPhone.

These few simple moments give a glimpse of me being able to access the world for information, social connection, and practical needs all in a blink of an eye, but progress did not stop there. Access became the spirit of the age. Technology became small and portable. People became mobile and connected.

These days, Myspace has been buried by the onslaught of social media that dominate our smartphones: Facebook, Twitter, Pinterest, Instagram, Snapchat, Twitch, and LinkedIn. I can follow my friends on their journeys across the world or across their living rooms. I can find new friends on the basis of common interests and likes. I can share my every thought on every item of the day, and I do not need to leave my bedroom and pj's to do it.

As connectivity grew, so did productivity. Email moved from desktop to laptop to iPhone. Offices migrated from corner office to corner coffee shop. Team meetings shifted from board rooms to Zoom rooms.

The ease of technology now dominates our day. Our smart speakers can control our lights, adjust our AC, or start our car. We can order food and have it delivered to our front steps in thirty minutes by a couple of taps on our phone. We can watch any movie on demand or binge watch our favorite show thanks to the power of streaming. No more waiting for a new episode to air next week and no more commercials.

So much of our lives has become quick and easy, and that is not all good. We have spent a generation being able to get what we want or need in the shortest amount of time possible. That ease is something we have grown used to. That ease has produced a term called "microwave mentality," which in essence means that if something cannot be done in five minutes or less, it is not worth doing.

Taken on its own merits, many of us would say we don't ascribe to the microwave mentality, but our behavior may say something different. Few of us enjoy the opportunity to exercise patience, and even fewer of us appreciate God answering a prayer with "Wait." We have been programmed to get things in our lives quickly and conveniently, which can be detrimental when it comes to our spiritual lives.

The Father does not work at the pace of our man-made culture. He does not count time like we count days. As Peter reminds us in 2 Peter 3:8, "But do not overlook this one fact, beloved, that with the Lord one day is as a thousand years, and a thousand years as one day." The Father does not conform His work to our broken perspective of time. He is not in a hurry; we are.

This is why it is vital for us to diagnose the hurried and impatient parts of our lives and conform them to the expectation that God has for His children. Often that expectation means us having to wait. God doesn't always move as quickly as our convenience-soaked hearts expect, and it is up to us to start the process of reprogramming our hearts to move at the speed of God. God's idea of the race He's set in front of us may not be at the pace we want, but it is exactly set at the pace we need. So let's take a few minutes to reorient our hurried hearts by looking at the character of God as our Creator and Sustainer.

GOD TAKES HIS TIME WITH HIS CLAY

> *But now, O LORD, you are our Father;*
> *we are the clay, and you are our potter;*
> *we are all the work of your hand.*
> **ISAIAH 64:8**

God as a potter and humanity as His clay or craftsmanship is a picture that we see quite a few times in Scripture. It evokes images of God as the kind and careful Creator but also as people being the work of God's hands. He is incredibly active with what He has made with His hands. He is not accidental in how He forms and fashions people, but deliberate.

We get a glimpse of this intentional craftsmanship in the first chapter of Scripture through an inter-Trinitarian conversation between the Father, Son, and Holy Spirit. They proclaim in Genesis 1:26, "Let us make man in our image, after our likeness." From that moment on, we see the declared purpose of why God made man: to display His image in all the world.

It is no wonder that God puts great care into how He puts together every child while they are still in their mother's womb—each baby is an image-bearer of their Maker. It is no wonder, with that clear purpose laid out for each child, that God takes His time fashioning us. As the psalmist reminds us in Psalm 139:13–14:

> For you formed my inward parts;
>   you knitted me together in my mother's womb.
> I praise you, for I am fearfully and wonderfully made.
> Wonderful are your works;
>   my soul knows it very well.

God goes to great lengths to form every one of His image-bearers who grace this earth. He is in no rush to cobble us together; rather, He makes us "fearfully and wonderfully." To put it another way, He makes us reverently and marvelously. He takes time with us so that His work may be made plain through us.

He crafts His children at conception in an extraordinarily careful way, but He does not stop there. The Potter continues to work His clay. He bends and molds. He forms spouts and handles. He adorns his pottery beyond the gray exterior. His great care in making us does not stop at conception.

His molding of us carries far beyond our infancy and into every aspect of our lives. The Christian can rejoice that "he who began a good work in you will bring it to completion at the day of Jesus Christ" (Philippians 1:6). God does not simply make you and then let you loose on your own to figure it out. He is set to work on you until the day that you see Him face to face.

That molding, refining, and maturing takes quite a bit of time. God is not in a rush to see His clay become a finished product, so we shouldn't be either. Realize that God has a timeline and plans in mind that will extend far beyond our immediate viewpoint. God does not work at the pace of culture; He works at the pace of eternity. The Potter is at work, and we must trust His unfolding, refining process for our lives. Because of Him, we wait, watch, and trust.

GOD IS IN CONTROL OF IT ALL

Has the potter no right over the clay, to make out
of the same lump one vessel for honorable use
and another for dishonorable use?
ROMANS 9:21

Again, we see the imagery of God as potter and people as the clay in Romans 9. This verse is a part of the greater conversation of the sovereign choice and work of God in Romans 9, which paints a broad, beautiful picture of the work of God in the world. He shows mercy to whom He wills. He makes one vessel for honorable use and crafts another for dishonor. He works as He wants for His glory.

For some, this is a difficult section to navigate. For others, it is a section of Scripture that is to be avoided altogether. When I was serving as a student pastor at a church years ago, our lead pastor was in the midst of a sermon series in the book of Romans. He had been in the series for months and had just finished a three-week span going through Romans 8—arguably the weightiest chapter in Scripture.

Following the last sermon in Romans 8, he picked up the series the next Sunday … in Romans 10. He had skipped Romans 9 completely, and I was shocked. You cannot exposit a book of the Bible by skipping an entire thirty-three verses, right? After the service I popped into his office, very curious to see why he had leapt over the chapter. I asked him outright, "Why did you skip Romans 9?"

"I didn't like what I read" was his only reply. I was stunned and had nothing to say in the wake of that comment. Romans 9 is a core passage for Calvinistic theology, and it is Scripture. It does not deserve to be shelved based on our preference.

There is great comfort in knowing that nothing escapes the grasp of God. Not only is He present in all things, but He is powerful in all things. He is working the best of days and the worst of days for His glory. There may be days that our apprehension and understanding of the work of God in our lives is unclear, but that doesn't negate the fact that He is on the move in our lives. He is at work in all things, and that is a good truth for us.

GOD WORKS ON AN ETERNAL TIMELINE FOR ETERNAL FRUIT

For this light momentary affliction is preparing for us an eternal weight of glory beyond all comparison, as we look not to the things that are seen but to the things that are unseen. For the things that are seen are transient, but the things that are unseen are eternal

2 CORINTHIANS 4:17–18

As we just saw, God is present and powerfully working in all things. He is sovereign and omnipotent. His work is ultimately eternal, and it does not fall apart or fade away. His permanence draws our eye in a world that seems to be fleeting.

Paul's reminder to the Corinthian church is to cast their vision beyond the horizon. We cannot look to the acts and goods of this world to give us any sort of permanence. The goods, the power, the acclaim, the momentum, and the money of this world all have a shelf life. One day they will fall to pieces and be given to someone else. Working for the tangible will only result in disappointment. Solomon puts it a little more strongly in Ecclesiastes 1:2–3:

> Vanity of vanities, says the Preacher,
> vanity of vanities! All is vanity.
> What does man gain by all the toil
> at which he toils under the sun?

Man toils for a lifetime by the work of his hands under the sun, and what does he have to show for it? Vanity. That certainly is harsh, but Solomon has experienced and tasted all the goods and glory of the world and he wants the reader to know it is not worth it. It will not last. It is all vanity.

Do we just stop living in this falling apart world? Not at all. We keep going with the life that the Father has kindly, sovereignly given us. We use the relationships, gifts, skills, and resources that we have to glorify Him. We use all the things of the world to show the world who He really is. The difference is where our hope lies. We live differently by loving the eternal things and seeing the temporary things for what they are.

We offer up this temporary life as a sacrifice to the One who has given it all to us in the first place. We give every bit of ourselves to God, knowing that is our one true means of worship. Worship is more than singing. It sees and savors the goodness and glory of God in our lives and in all of creation, even while God's work in us is not finished. We look at those graces and we love His glory, knowing that is the reason why the Potter molded this little bit of human clay in the first place.

We can enjoy so much of the convenience that the twenty-first century has brought us without becoming trapped in the microwave mentality that the culture has formed. We can push back against the pressure of living hurried, right-now-oriented lives, and one of our greatest weapons that God has given us in this fight is the chance to reflect on His eternal character. Our lives seem saner and make infinitely more sense when viewed through the lens of God's eternal and sovereign plan.

With that plan in mind, we must be faithful to take a step back from our busy lives to consider what we have in our loving Father. We need to give ourselves the space to soak in the fact that our Creator and Savior love us dearly. We must carve out pockets in the day to stop and commune with the eternal God beyond the space of our Sundays.

The psalmist gives us this poignant reminder in Psalm 46:10: "Be still, and know that I am God. I will be exalted among the nations, I will be exalted in the earth!" When we are still, we see God for who He is. Our busyness crowds out our perception of His grace, movement, and purpose that He is producing in our lives. If we would take a few minutes to simply stop and be still, we could grasp the character of God expressed toward us and His sovereign work in us.

If we still our hearts before God and soak in His character, He is faithful to help us see and endure the long race that lays before us.

CHAPTER 2

HOW TO RUN WITHOUT RELENTING

Blessed is the man who remains steadfast under trial, for when he has stood the test he will receive the crown of life, which God has promised to those who love him.

JAMES 1:12

I can remember the moment like it was yesterday, even though it has been almost ten years now. I had just finished preaching at a community-wide youth event in Wilson, North Carolina, called Youth Week. More than a dozen youth groups from all across our city gathered to grow in Christ and share the gospel with lost students. It was an honor to be a part of something that brought the gospel to hundreds of students in our community.

At this point in my ministry, I had only a couple video recordings of me preaching. The church I spoke at for Youth Week had a dedicated audio-visual team who recorded the sermon and uploaded it to YouTube. It was incredible to have my sermon out there for me to be able to share with my family and friends. I searched for my sermon and clicked the link on YouTube to start watching.

As I popped up on the screen, I noticed one thing immediately. I looked a little doughy. I knew I had put on a little bit of weight, but this was no longer just a *little*. It was a LOT. There was no hiding my protruding gut on my tiny frame. I needed to find a way to be more physically active and get my body in a healthier place.

I started by joining an adult soccer league in our city. I had played soccer growing up and figured that would be the perfect place to start. Playing made me more active and I was definitely enjoying myself, but there were two problems. The first problem was the short season. We only played one day a week for six weeks. It was a lot of running on one day but that was it. The second problem was our league was full of guys who played Division I and even professional soccer overseas. I last played organized soccer as an eleven-year-old at the YMCA. I was clearly out of my league.

With my soccer career coming into early retirement, I had to find another way to get my fitness in a better place, but I did not know where to start. One of my best friends, Brad, had an idea of what I could do. Brad was a youth pastor in Wilson and had preached at Youth Week, so he had seen my doughiness up close. He told me about this thing called CrossFit.

Brad had found CrossFit and had amazing results. I figured that it would not hurt to check the place out. I spent my first few days trying to figure out how to do CrossFit without arms. Many of the movements and lifts depend on having hands, so there were some adaptions that needed to be made. My trainer knew exactly what to do and how to adapt exercises so that no hands were needed. In no time I was doing back squats, dead lifts, kettlebell swings, and push-ups. I had the basics out of the way, and it was time for my first real CrossFit workout.

I showed up at the gym the next day, excited for my very first WOD (workout of the day), but my heart quickly sank. CrossFit has several WODs called "Hero WODs" that are named after a fallen soldier to honor their memory and sacrifice. These WODs are intentionally put together to be absolutely brutal workouts in order to illustrate the sacrifices made by these fallen men and women.

My first workout was a Hero WOD named "Griff," in honor of US Air Force Sergeant Travis Griffin, who was killed in 2008. The actual workout was simple: two rounds of an 800-meter run and a 400-meter backward run. But there was one important caveat: I am not a runner.

The clock sounded, and off we went. The first 800-meter run was not great, but I found a way to grind through it. Then came the backward run, which I assumed would feel just like running forward but in a different direction. Nope.

Turns out, running backward works a completely different set of muscles. I took off and my lungs started to sting a little, but I figured that was because I was fresh off of running a half mile. Then a sharp, burning sensation started in my calves and quickly worked its way up my legs into my quads and my hamstrings. I finished the first round of the WOD at a snail's pace. I was only halfway through, but I was gasping for air and my legs were shaking.

The next fifteen minutes were a bit of a blur. There were a few stops along the way to catch my breath and another few because my legs stung so badly. Once I finally reached the finish line, I plopped down onto the concrete. I was spent, but I had finished the workout. But the workout was not finished with me.

I went through the rest of my day and then went to bed that night. I woke up the next morning and my legs felt like concrete. Everything from my hips down ached and felt as stiff as granite. My legs were so sore that I struggled to get my foot to my mouth so I could eat my breakfast.

That workout exposed a lot about me and my fitness. First off, my gut was not the only problem. My entire body was out of shape, including my legs—the part of my body that I accomplish the majority of my daily tasks with. The second thing I realized was that I had a really long way to go if I wanted to get in better shape. There would be many more workouts and a whole lot more pain before I reached my fitness goals. This was not a quick fix. Did I want to do what it took to get there?

My first exposure to CrossFit is reminiscent of the early days of my journey as a disciple of Jesus—with obvious differences. Jesus had already won my victory through His death and resurrection. He had already placed His Holy Spirit in my heart as a seal of my salvation. By His work I was adopted as a son and brought into the family of God so that I would no longer be a slave to my sin and lusts. He buried my old man in His death and brought a new man to life in His resurrection.

Jesus accomplished the unthinkable through His life and death so that I might have a new life in Him. With all the work He had done and all the victories He had won for me, Jesus's plea was now: "Take up your cross. Deny yourself. Follow me." He was calling me to discipleship, but as I looked around, I realized that the road to following Jesus was long and hard. This was not going to be a quick trip. Did I want to do what it took to follow my Lord?

This is what many people describe as "counting the cost" of discipleship. The grace of the gospel was costly to the Father as He gave His Son to buy back broken sinners like you and me. That sort of cost to God means grace cannot be taken advantage of. Grace comes with a call and cost as well. Dietrich Bonhoeffer put it this way: "Such grace is costly because it calls us to follow, and it is grace because it calls us to follow Jesus Christ. It is costly because it costs a man his life, and it is grace because it gives a man the only true life."[1]

Our reply to the grace of the gospel should not come with a half-hearted yes. The call to "follow me" cannot be a shuffling after Jesus. We respond to Him with our whole-hearted yes at all times. We follow Him with full awareness of the long and hard road ahead, with a daily step-by-step pursuit.

The call to follow Jesus is not an Olympic 100-meter sprint. This is not nine seconds of the absolute best we have and then we can try again in four years. To be a disciple of Jesus is a lifetime commitment to follow Jesus in every season of life through every circumstance imaginable. This is the ultimate display of endurance.

That call is really intimidating. I am in my mid-thirties, and Lord willing, I have a few more decades left on this earth. To follow Jesus means I need to trust Him with my kids getting their driver's licenses, with my children's marriages, with my grand-kids, with my ministry, with my retirement, and with everything else in between.

That is incredibly scary because I know that there is so much more tucked in between those touchstone moments of life. I have many more struggles, sins, hurts, trials, and tragedies to navigate before my race is fully run. The weight of everything that lays in front of me pushes my heart to tap out now before I take another step.

How can we get to the place where we can be as content as Paul when he hit the homestretch in his faith race? As he says in 2 Timothy 4:7, "I have fought the good fight, I have finished the race, I have kept the faith." He followed his Savior with all that he had, and he was ready to see the Lord that he loved face to face.

How do we fight and run without relenting? Let's look at Scripture for some answers.

DROP THE DEAD WEIGHT

Therefore, since we are surrounded by so great a cloud of witnesses, let us also lay aside every weight, and sin which clings so closely, and let us run with endurance the race that is set before us, looking to Jesus, the founder and perfecter of our faith, who for the joy that was set before him endured the cross, despising the shame, and is seated at the right hand of the throne of God.

HEBREWS 12:1-2

Coming on the heels of what many call the Hall of Fame of Faith in Hebrews 11, the author points the reader back to the faithful followers' examples one more time. With that great list of faithful men and women before you, push aside all the sin and all the weight that life throws at you, just like they did. These faithful people had sins like lying, murder, adultery, and prostitution in their pasts, but by the grace of God they turned from them and pursued Him.

There are plenty of excuses they could have offered God for why they did not need to run their race of faith. Abraham had every good thing the world had to offer. Why did he need to give that up to obey God? Moses was on the short list of most powerful people on the planet. Why did he need to relinquish his throne for the sake of some Jewish slaves? Yet, Moses accepted God's call to lead a million people to freedom, but who would follow a man that was slow of speech? Rahab was already branded as a whore. Why would God's people want to trust her?

The list of excuses for why God could not use these faithful people would fill a book. Yet, for a God that parts seas, slays undefeated giants, drops indestructible walls, and calls dead people to life, the excuses of humanity are feeble in light of His inexhaustible strength. He simply asks that you trust Him with the weakest parts of who you are, and He will make His strength evident.

God knows the race that lays in front of you. He knows all your inadequacies and insecurities. He knows the trials that are waiting for you that you cannot foresee. He knows all your past failures and your failures to come, and He promises to be your strength when you are broken. As Isaiah says in Isaiah 40:31, "But they who wait for the LORD shall renew their strength; they shall mount up with wings like eagles; they shall run and not be weary; they shall walk and not faint."

The weight of your weakness is cast off by the might of God, and your sins are removed by the grace of God. If we confess our sins, we know that the Father is faithful to forgive them (1 John 1:9). If we are entangled by our sin, we can ask the Spirit to put to death the deeds of our flesh (Romans 8:13). Jesus founds our faith in the power of the cross and is the perfecter of that faith by removing all the entanglements that sin chokes us with.

All of the weight of excuse and disobedience is lifted by the work of Christ, and He asks that we fix our eyes on Him to see this race through. Focus on Him and look to Him and it will be Christ who will get you to the finish line of faith. There is a Hall of Fame of Faith filled with servants of Jesus who can testify to His sustaining grace.

DO WHAT IS NEXT

Do you not know that in a race all the runners run, but only one receives the prize? So run that you may obtain it. Every athlete exercises self-control in all things. They do it to receive a perishable wreath, but we an imperishable. So I do not run aimlessly; I do not box as one beating the air.

1 CORINTHIANS 9:24-26

Here is another sports analogy. Stick with me here. Paul, like the author of Hebrews, makes the comparison between our spiritual lives and a race. For runners, they run with one purpose in mind. Boxers come into the ring with their sights set on their opponent on the other side of the ring.

So also for believers, we do not run this endurance race without a purpose in mind. We run this race with the ultimate goal of bringing honor and glory to Christ. In every aspect of our lives we seek to glorify the One who saved us. As 1 Corinthians 10:31 proclaims, "So, whether you eat or drink, or whatever you do, do all to the glory of God."

As I look across the landscape and timeline of my life, it seems overwhelming to do *everything* to the glory of God. Over the years I have had to make big choices, like where and how to serve in ministry, as well as small choices, like when I should have an evangelistic conversation with a lost friend. Having the freedom to choose what and where to go can have a paralyzing effect on a person. One of my favorite fast-food places in North Carolina is called Cook Out. It has all sorts of burgers, hot dogs, and sandwiches, but its specialty is milkshakes. They have more than forty milkshake flavors, including Snickers, banana, pineapple, mint Oreo, M&M, fresh watermelon, and even eggnog. Every time I walk in, I find myself frozen just trying to navigate the milkshake menu. How much more when faced with *everything* in my life? So it is when it comes to glorifying God in the broad expanse of our lives. We look around at all the possibilities we can pursue, but the endless choices can freeze us where we stand. Trying to discern what is good from what is best is challenging, but we cannot allow that to muddle our pursuit of Christ.

Often the best thing we can do is simply the next right thing. Before you accuse me of expounding theology from *Frozen II*, hear me out. There are gigantic crossroads that we come across in our lives. They present decisions like what to major in, where to work, where to live, what church to attend, what ministry to support, or even what gospel opportunities to personally pursue. In these circumstances we might pray, seek wisdom and counsel, and weigh all the options. Sometimes the process takes weeks or even years.

As we wait to decide, that does not mean that we take a break from our faith lives. While we wait, we still need to serve, love, and proclaim in whatever place life finds us. We capital-ize on the opportunities that some may see as small, knowing there is so much more that God has in store for us. Discerning what is next does not have to deter us from doing anything; it just allows us to follow the detours in life.

Hudson Taylor describes it like this: "A little thing is a little thing, but faithfulness in little things is a great thing."[2] Taylor is arguably one of the most prolific missionaries in the last three hundred years as he brought over eight hundred missionar-ies into China and directly saw more than eighteen thousand people trust Jesus as Lord during his fifty-one years as head of China Inland Mission.[3] His work was monumental when viewed over the course of a lifetime, but it can be boiled down to a multitude of faithful moments with a singular aim.

The challenge Jesus gives His disciples through the parable of the dishonest manager in Luke 16:10 accentuates this call: "One who is faithful in a very little is also faithful in much, and one who is dishonest in a very little is also dishonest in much." This truth is echoed in the parable of talents in Matthew 25:21: "His master said to him, 'Well done, good and faithful servant. You have been faithful over a little; I will set you over much. Enter into the joy of your master.' "

Even if you are in a place where you feel like your gospel opportunity is tiny, do not despise these small moments of faithfulness. A lifetime of small, faithful moments adds up to showing the world an immensely faithful God behind it all.

DO NOT QUIT

And let us not grow weary of doing good, for in due season
we will reap, if we do not give up.
GALATIANS 6:9

When I run for exercise, quitting seems like a valid option about 90 percent of the time. Who in their right mind would want to put themselves through something like this? The sweating, the burning lungs, the sore legs—it is all awful.

We could say the same thing about being a disciple of Jesus. Who in their right mind would want to put themselves through something like this? Having to love your neighbors and pray for your enemies—has the Lord seen what they write on Facebook? I have to submit to my authorities and pray for them? Has God seen these guys who walk into the White House?

Loving God and others is hard when the easiest person to love is myself. The relationships closest to us can be the most draining, but those relationships can also be the most rewarding. To those people we can give the pure, unfiltered love of Jesus. We can love them simply because we know that Jesus loves them. They do not have to be perfect or act perfectly; I just cannot weary of displaying Jesus's love to them.

Weariness of doing good is a real symptom of living in a world that tears one another apart. People can be hard, but so are our lives. It seems like every corner we turn or every milestone we hit, there is also evidence of the brokenness sin has left in its wake.

From the fall of man in Genesis 3, humanity has been set to deal with toil, frustration, hurt, strife, and ultimately death. The proclamation of hurt and death in Genesis 3 also came with a hopeful promise that One was coming to crush the head and deeds of the garden serpent. Even with that hope, we groan like Paul says in Romans 8:23: "And not only the creation, but we ourselves, who have the firstfruits of the Spirit, groan inwardly as we wait eagerly for adoption as sons, the redemption of our bodies."

Groaning has a cumulative effect in our minds and hearts. The inner turmoil of doubt, shame, fear, and discord closes off our hearts. We pull inward and away from the people we love the most. Our outer trials and hurt land like body blows on our already weary life. There are extended seasons of life where it seems like nothing can go right. We are enveloped in darkness and the only thing we want is to lie down and quit.

It is the same temptation to quit that Elijah came face to face with in 1 Kings 19. God had just defeated the prophets of Baal by raining down fire on Mount Carmel. Following their defeat, the false prophets were killed, which was not something Jezebel appreciated. She swore to have Elijah killed in the next twenty-four hours.

As soon as Elijah heard of the threat he went out into the desert, curled up under a tree, and asked to die. This was a quick drop to go from the most powerful prophet in Israel to being pushed to the absolute brink. Even a man who had seen God do unimaginably powerful acts found himself overwhelmed by his fear.

God did not scold or scoff at Elijah; rather, He sent an angel to attend to him. This angel gave Elijah food and water and then let Elijah go back to sleep. The angel returned a second time to give food and drink to Elijah so that he would have strength for his journey ahead. Then God sent him to a mountain where He showed Elijah both His power and His tenderness.

God never scolded Elijah for succumbing to his hurt and fear. His response to Elijah was one of tender provision. God provided the rest and the strength that Elijah needed. God reminded the prophet that the presence of the Father was never far from him. He was with him, for him, and still had plans for him.

God is not done with you. Until faith becomes sight, God desires to uphold you, love you, and use you as an instrument of His glory. The ultimate antidote to our fears and failures is that God's presence in our lives is not dependent on present success; it is an established promise to His children. As the prophet Isaiah reminds vulnerable Israel:

> You are my servant,
>> I have chosen you and not cast you off;
>> fear not, for I am with you;
>> be not dismayed, for I am your God;
> I will strengthen you, I will help you,
>> I will uphold you with my righteous right hand.
>> (Isaiah 41:9–10)

A sovereign and powerful God is not dismayed by your darkness, struggles, and failures. He knows about all of it, and He still loves you. He is still beside you and sustaining you. Take time to recover from your wounds. Take time to rest in His arms of grace. Build your strength as you trust in Him.

But eventually, get back up. Do not stop running the race, even if that means going one small step at a time. It might be hard, but God has you in His hand. Do not quit. God has made you for more than fear and failure.

We know it is a hard and long journey, but with God at our side, we can run the race one step at a time until we reach the finish line of faith.

Over the next few chapters, we'll look at some rhythms that will help us run with endurance, but before we look at those rhythms, I want to put this caveat in here: as you read, please do not assume that these rhythms are prescriptive. They are descriptive of healthy acts we can place in our lives on a consistent basis. These do not have to happen every day of every week for you to grow in Christ. I have no desire for this to be a legalistic checklist that you have to do.

Throughout the course of this book, we'll walk through rhythms that you can practice on your own and within community to build endurance for the long run of faith, starting with Scripture, extending to lament and prayer, and then turning to local church membership, family, witness, and discipleship. Along the way, three case studies will allow us to look more closely at the examples of Paul, Abraham, and Joseph, whose lives of faith illustrate endurance and trust in God.

The suggestions in the chapters to come are for your encouragement and equipping. May these rhythms help you look more like Jesus so that the world may see Jesus in you.

PAUL

THE GRACE TO ENDURE

Now I would remind you, brothers, of the gospel I preached
to you, which you received, in which you stand, and by which
you are being saved, if you hold fast to the word I preached
to you—unless you believed in vain.
1 CORINTHIANS 15:1-2

The apostle Paul was a man that God used in massive ways
in the founding, establishing, and forward movement of
the church. God used him to pen more of the New Testament
than any other person. God charged Paul with the establishing
of the gentile church, sending him all across the Mediterranean
region to lay the seeds of the gospel and plant churches in a
number of major cities.

His influence remains to this day. Many pastors and theo-
logians will say, apart from Christ, Paul stands as the most
influential figure in their ministry. All sorts of aspects of Paul's
life and ministry can encourage us: the boldness and clarity
with which he preached and wrote; the centrality of Christ in
everything that Paul said and did. Many people I know love
Paul because of the intense love he showed the people of God.

I wholeheartedly agree with all those attributes. My ministry has been shaped deeply by what God did through the life of Paul. I am encouraged and challenged by his orthodoxy and his orthopraxy. Yet one thing above all others has drawn me to Paul: the constant endurance he showed in the face of trials.

Many are encouraged by Paul's theology, but I am encouraged and challenged by Paul's pain. His pain at times was an extreme bother to him (his thorn in the flesh), but he continued to press on in view of both the grace of God and the call of God on his life. When others saw brokenness and woe, Paul saw the grace of God present in his life and ministry: "But by the grace of God I am what I am, and his grace toward me was not in vain. On the contrary, I worked harder than any of them, though it was not I, but the grace of God that is with me" (1 Corinthians 15:10).

I have turned to this verse over and over again for the past twenty years of trusting Jesus as Lord. I have often battled the thought that my armlessness is the greatest curse in my life, but the biblical truth is far from that. My disability was not caused by any sort of genetic mutation or accident in the womb. I was born this way by the sovereign grace and design of God.

As I began to view my lack of arms through the lens of the grace of God, everything about my life changed. I no longer moped about my condition or people's perception of it. I realized that God had given me a gift that few others had. God gave me an external appearance that catches the attention and curiosity of others. As people pause to get a closer look at my armless state, they also notice a hope and joy that I have—and that does not make worldly sense. How could a man that looks like that have a hope like that?

I watch people processing my disability alongside my joy—and so they ask, "Why are you so happy?" In that conversation I get to tell them about the grace of God in my life. The grace that saved me. The grace that gives me strength to endure amid my trials and frustrations. The grace that my disability affords me to have conversations with curious passersby that people with arms never get to have. By the grace of God, I am afforded the chance to enjoy this life He has given me, and I will not let it go to waste. Grace pushes me forward when life wants to drag me down.

The grace of God also pushed Paul forward in the face of unrelenting pressure, persecution, and trial. Grace pulled him through unimaginable circumstances, and it is that same grace that will allow us to endure whatever may come our way.

AN IDENTITY-SHAPING GRACE

The grace, gospel, and glory of God was everything to Paul. He attributed nothing to his talent, abilities, or sheer will. God gave Paul every good thing he had ever known. Paul was not a casual fan of Jesus. The person and the work of Christ was everything to him. That is why he can boldly and unequivocally say in Philippians 1:20–21: "As it is my eager expectation and hope that I will not be at all ashamed, but that with full courage now as always Christ will be honored in my body, whether by life or by death. For to me to live is Christ, and to die is gain."

As long as Paul was in the flesh, he was going to live every waking minute to bring Jesus glory. When he finished his earthly race, he was just as excited and passionate because he would get to see his Savior face to face. It did not matter whether he was before King Agrippa or King Jesus, Christ was Paul's everything, and he wanted to be certain that everyone else knew it.

Paul's life was not about to be used for temporal purposes played out in a fleeting world. His days were spent and poured out for the eternal, lasting purposes of the one true King of heaven and earth. Christ was both Paul's purpose and his reward.

That identity-founding reality of the gospel of God is a cosmic kindness. God is kind enough to give you and me a purpose that does not wither. The treasures from the storehouse of our King do not erode. His kingdom is never threatened, and His purposes will never be thwarted. This everlasting and unrelenting identity as a disciple is what allows followers of Christ to not be shaken.

A GRACE THAT ABSORBS THE LOSS OF ALL THINGS

But whatever gain I had, I counted as loss for the sake of Christ. Indeed, I count everything as loss because of the surpassing worth of knowing Christ Jesus my Lord. For his sake I have suffered the loss of all things and count them as rubbish, in order that I may gain Christ.

PHILIPPIANS 3:7-9

In worldly terms, one of the worst things that ever happened to Paul was his conversion on the road to Damascus. Before encountering Jesus on that road, Paul had everything the world values: wealth, power, self-righteousness, and fame. The moment he met Christ that all changed.

He was disowned by the Jewish elite. Christians feared him so much that they wanted nothing to do with him. He struggled as a tentmaker to make ends meet while he began his ministry of getting the gospel to the gentiles. He was beaten, mocked, imprisoned, and stoned—all for the sake of the gospel that he proclaimed to the world. And what was Paul's response?

"It was worth it. I would lose it all again that I may know Jesus as my Lord."

The grace of God is a treasure that easily outweighs all earthly riches and power. Whereas wealth must be accrued, grace is freely given. Whereas riches are given away at death, the inheritance of believers is granted to them the moment they trust Jesus as Lord (Ephesians 1:13–14). Whereas the possessions of this world lose their luster, the treasure in our earthen vessels shines for the span of our Christian life.

What we have in the grace of Christ is a gift that stands head and shoulders above anything else the world has to offer. His grace is sufficient to fill every bit of the basic needs that a person can ever have. In Him we can lose it all and say that He is enough. He is better than the pleasure and powers that use us.

He is our greatest aim and hope because He is the One we were made for. He gives life where the enemy wants to rob us of it (John 10:10). As the world seeks to make a name for itself, Christ graciously gives us life in His name. He is everything we could want and then more. He is our prize, our aim, our everything.

THE GRACE OF AFFLICTION

So to keep me from becoming conceited because of the surpassing greatness of the revelations, a thorn was given me in the flesh, a messenger of Satan to harass me, to keep me from becoming conceited. Three times I pleaded with the Lord about this, that it should leave me. But he said to me, "My grace is sufficient for you, for my power is made perfect in weakness." Therefore I will boast all the more gladly of my weaknesses, so that the power of Christ may rest upon me. For the sake of Christ, then, I am content with weaknesses, insults, hardships, persecutions, and calamities.
For when I am weak, then I am strong.
2 CORINTHIANS 12:7-10

There is a lot of speculation as to what exactly Paul's thorn in the flesh was, but we do know it was enough of an issue that Paul pleaded with God multiple times for it to go away. Paul's pleading was not heeded by the Lord. Rather God tells Paul that what happened to him was something that would work out for the good of Paul and the glory of God. This affliction was an act of grace in order that the power of God may be fully displayed in his life.

In the economy of the gospel, even our hardships can be blessings that God sends our way. When our weaknesses throb in our soul like a deep bruise, we have the opportunity to fully taste a power that cannot come from human strength, which is God's point to Paul. By peeling away the years Paul had spent seeking to be self-righteous and self-sufficient, Paul was able to clearly see his frailty and God's power.

The grace of God works in our lives to wreck the lie the serpent uttered in the garden. The lure of being like God pulled Adam and Eve into the fall of man, so God provided us with a reminder that we are not and never will be Him—our weaknesses. One of God's great graces to us are the weaknesses and trials of this life. They expose the lie of self-sufficiency while shining a light on our God who lacks nothing.

Our afflictions, though painful and wearisome, can be a tool that God uses to show us more of Himself. By our trials we are able to both fully know and share in the comfort of God (2 Corinthians 1:3–11). Also in the fires of trial, we come to know who we are while God molds and shapes us. Peter calls us to rejoice in our trials (1 Peter 1:6–7) as our precious faith is being refined in order to bring praise, glory, and honor to Christ.

When trials and afflictions come with all sorts of pain, anxiety, and fear, know that we do not suffer without hope because God is redeeming our worst experiences for both our good and His glory. Hope and boast in those hard times, for when we are at our worst, the Creator and Sustainer of the world is at His best.

TRUE FRIENDS ARE A GRACE
ONLY GOD CAN GIVE

Paul met a multitude of people during his ministry. Some came into his life because they were curious and wanted to know more about this Savior he constantly talked about. Others came into Paul's life because they felt threatened by him and the gospel he espoused.

Only a few linked arms with Paul in his gospel mission. These people helped fund him, prayed for him, served alongside him, and waged spiritual war against the darkness. Paul's life is littered with people like John Mark, Timothy, Barnabas, and Lydia—people that Paul had a deep-seated affection for: "I thank God whom I serve, as did my ancestors, with a clear conscience, as I remember you constantly in my prayers night and day. As I remember your tears, I long to see you, that I may be filled with joy. I am reminded of your sincere faith, a faith that dwelt first in your grandmother Lois and your mother Eunice and now, I am sure, dwells in you as well" (2 Timothy 1:3–4).

These first few verses of 2 Timothy give us a glimpse into what Paul really thought about Timothy. We can tell the two men knew each other well, and Paul longed for the day that he could see his friend and co-laborer again. Yet, this is not a novel thing for Paul. The introductions of many of his epistles show his love for those he knows as he prays and weeps over a body of believers. For as bold and mythic as the apostle Paul seems, he saw the people of God as true treasure and grace.

A brother or sister who can encourage you, labor beside you, and love you at all costs is a rare thing. For all the glorious trinkets that the world can dangle in front of you, little can compete with the love and grace that comes from the relationships Christ has strung together in His church. Do not take graces like that for granted. A true brother or sister in the faith is precisely what you need as you navigate the valleys and mountains of this life. Celebrate these relationships for what they are—true gifts from God that are freely given by His grace.

THE GRACE TO STAND STRONG

To this day I have had the help that comes from God, and so I stand here testifying both to small and great, saying nothing but what the prophets and Moses said would come to pass: that the Christ must suffer and that, by being the first to rise from the dead, he would proclaim light both to our people and to the Gentiles.

ACTS 26:22-23

Paul grew accustomed to opposition to his ministry and to the gospel itself. By the end of Acts, Paul is being dragged all around, appearing before tribunals and councils to plead for both his freedom and his life. In Acts 26, Paul makes an appeal before King Agrippa in order to gain his freedom.

As Paul deals with the false claims Jewish leadership has made against him, he does not waste an opportunity to proclaim the gospel that put him in this position in the first place. As he stands before some of the most powerful people in the region, Paul is fearless in making sure that King Agrippa knows the work of Christ crucified and resurrected.

Paul is in a situation where the stakes could not be higher, and God gives him both the strength and the words that he needs. The grace of God in high pressure moments is not only granted to the superstars of the New Testament like Paul. The assistance of the Holy Spirit is promised to all who take up their cross and follow Christ: "And when they bring you before the synagogues and the rulers and the authorities, do not be anxious about how you should defend yourself or what you should say, for the Holy Spirit will teach you in that very hour what you ought to say" (Luke 12:11–12).

Just as the Holy Spirit stepped in to give Paul the words to say, he promises to help us too. We may never be before actual courts where our freedom or life hangs in the balance, but the day is already here when Christian belief is on trial in the court of public opinion. The Christian call to be in the world but not of the world (John 17:14) and the world's adoption of cancel culture are at odds with one another. The Christian does not have the same worldview, values, or way of life that the world does.

This tension places Christians under scrutiny due to the way we live for and love God. In these moments of incongruity, we are given an opportunity to speak about why we do what we do and the hope that God has given us in His gospel. This is not something that casually happens. This is a reality that Scripture has called the disciple to be prepared for: "But even if you should suffer for righteousness' sake, you will be blessed. Have no fear of them, nor be troubled, but in your hearts honor Christ the Lord as holy, always being prepared to make a defense to anyone who asks you for a reason for the hope that is in you; yet do it with gentleness and respect" (1 Peter 3:14–15).

The strain between the kingdom of God and the kingdom of humanity places the Christian under constant scrutiny. This does not have to be anything we fear but something we can expect as strangers and aliens in this world. Like Paul in Philippians 1, the suffering of this world leaves us with dual desires: pursuing Christ on this earth in the midst of pain and longing to be with Christ in eternity. Yet, even as we brace for what may come, we know we have a gracious God who is with us all the way—giving us strength to stand and words to say.

CHAPTER 3

READ THE WORD

Your word is a lamp to my feet and a light to my path.
PSALM 119:105

In the first few weeks of being a believer, there was one verse I turned to day after day after day: Philippians 4:13, which says, "I can do all things through him who strengthens me." This Scripture breathed so much life into me in those early days of my faith. For a life that had been immersed in so much failure, it was an enormous comfort to know that God would be my source of strength even in my times of weakness.

That one verse was such a boost for me, and in a lot of ways, it had become *my verse*. It was a verse that I leaned on but also one that I was ready to share whenever the opportunity presented itself. I preached "I Can Do All Things" mini sermons to anyone who was willing to listen. As the days went by, I noticed a couple of things about how I was treating Scripture.

First, I was clinging to one piece of Scripture as my source of spiritual food, and that was not enough. It was like eating Doritos for every bit of sustenance for weeks on end. It may taste good, but the human body is not made to live on corn chips doused with powdered cheese. Junk food is really tasty, but a balanced diet is a great foundation for a healthy life.

The same is true for how we consume Scripture. It is amazing when we have a single verse or a handful of verses that we can turn to in times where we need encouragement and sustenance. That was me; I had a rock of a verse to turn to whenever I needed it, but I was ignoring other sections of Scripture that were just as beautiful, powerful, and life-changing.

The second thing I took note of was that my understanding of who God was and how He was moving in my life was very uneven. I kept focusing on God as my supplier of strength, but what about His work in giving me hope or mercy? I was lacking in my understanding of His gospel and what it meant for me as one now adopted into the family of God. How was I supposed to act as a child of God? I realized that I had access to the living and breathing Word of God, but I was choosing to focus on only a tiny part of the whole.

I needed to spend more time in the Bible and get to know all that God had placed in His Word, but I had absolutely no clue where to start or how to study the Bible. I knew how to study American history, but I had no idea how to study the precepts of God. Like any other kid, if I did not understand something, I asked my mom. She had been a believer since childhood and had taught others the Scriptures in Sunday School classes and in women's Bible studies for as long as I could remember.

My mom and I sat down one afternoon, and she laid out how she studied the Bible. She explained to me how to move through one book of the Bible in small chunks. She showed me the different English translations of the Bible and how to use helpful resources like study notes, cross-references, and commentaries. She talked to me about the importance of writing down what God was teaching me so that I could come back to it at a later time.

We could not have been there for more than an hour, but my mom's crash course on studying the Bible was a launching point for my faith. That night, I began to study the book of Philippians, and the letter from Paul to the church at Philippi took on a whole new life in my eyes. I was blown away by the persistent work of Christ through His church that He loved dearly. I saw the humility of Christ taking on flesh and being crucified as a criminal and the call for the believer to have that same mindset. I learned that having Christ as my greatest treasure means that everything the world has is trash in comparison to knowing Jesus as my everything. I realized I can do all things through Christ—for His glory and not my own.

This regular rhythm of making Scripture a vital part of my life set me on a course to grow as a disciple of Jesus, and it also sharpened me into the pastor that I would be one day. God was using the parts of my life then to set me on a path to look more like Jesus while also giving me the means to share the hope of Jesus with the listening world. His Word was the spiritual food (1 Corinthians 3:2) helping me to mature in the faith while also allowing me to know more of the God who had saved me.

If we are aiming to endure in our faith, we need the fuel that will help us run the long race that stretches in front of us. What can we do to get a steady diet of Scripture into our lives?

READ THE WORD

There are many of us who do not fancy ourselves as readers. We are not the type who take seven books on vacation to read at the beach, and we do not plan our office space around where our bookshelves will go. However, the majority of us do read small bits of information on a daily basis. We will look at sport scores and athlete interviews on our favorite sports app. We will read through our friends' posts and tweets every night before we go to bed. We check the weather report for the coming week.

We do these things for the sake of familiarity. We want to know what our favorite football player did in Sunday's game and why he made the decisions that he did to win the game. We read the status updates of our friends or we watch their stories on Instagram so we can know what is going on in their lives. It gives us a glimpse of what they are doing, where they are going, or what they are learning.

We have the same opportunity to become familiar with the God who loves us by reading His Word. He loves us so much that He gave us the Bible so that we can begin to understand His character, His promises, His gospel, and His call for us to live as His disciples. His Word is a powerful means to get to know God in all His fullness.

As the author of Hebrews states in 4:12, "For the word of God is living and active, sharper than any two-edged sword, piercing to the division of soul and of spirit, of joints and of marrow, and discerning the thoughts and intentions of the heart." The Word of God is a sword in the hands of the believer. It is a weapon that needs to be handled and used. As warriors and soldiers spend countless hours getting familiar with the tool that will keep them safe and bring them victory, so Christians ought to familiarize themselves with the weapon that God has provided for instruction and edification.

Find ways to read God's Word regularly. Read a chapter or two while you drink coffee in the morning. Open your Bible app and read at night before you open your social media apps. A plethora of apps exist for your phone that provide Scripture anywhere you are. Two very helpful apps are *He Reads Truth* for men or *She Reads Truth* for women. The access that the Western world has to Scripture leaves us without excuse—we must find time to familiarize ourselves with God's Word.

STUDY THE BIBLE

Casually reading through Scripture has a tremendous amount of value for the believer, but so does careful study of it. We read to familiarize ourselves with the God we serve, but we study so that we start to grasp the depth of both God and His gospel. We love the God who saved us by giving ourselves to the studying of what He has revealed about Himself. As it says in Luke 10:27, "You shall love the Lord your God with all your heart and with all your soul and with all your strength and with all your mind, and your neighbor as yourself." Our study of the Bible is a way we love God with all our mind.

As I shared earlier in the chapter, starting to study Scripture on your own is intimidating. I had no idea where to start or what tools to use as I got into studying the Bible. I am so thankful that my mom took time to lay out how I can do it on my own. I certainly have learned a few tips since then, but she helped me to get going in the right direction.

Now, I do not have an unassailable framework for studying the Bible, and many other people have great advice on how to study it. However, I want to lay out a few of the basics so that you can start studying the Bible on your own if you have not already made that a part of your life.

1. *Get a readable translation of the Bible*—We live in a day where there are several English translations of the Bible. Some prefer translations like the King James Version, but for others, it can be an obstacle because of the historical English. I recommend

getting a Bible translation that is easy to read but is also a literal translation. Some translations—NIV, The Message, NLT—are thought-by-thought translations, which are helpful for casual reading but not necessarily for study. Three of the translations that I study and preach from are the English Standard Version (ESV), the Christian Standard Bible (CSB), and the New American Standard Bible (NASB).

2. *Get a study Bible or a commentary*—There are numerous portions of Scripture where understanding the context of what is being described or taught is crucial. There are also portions of Scripture that are just difficult to understand. The great news is that there are study Bibles and commentaries that can help us understand the context of Scripture while also providing explanations of difficult passages. You can buy commentaries that cover the whole Bible or commentaries that help explain a particular book of the Bible. One of my favorite commentaries for the whole Bible is the *Tyndale Concise Bible Commentary*, and my favorite commentary series for specific books of the Bible is the Christ-Centered Exposition series. If you prefer digital commentaries and Bibles, Logos Bible Software is an amazing tool, as well as the free app, Logos Bible Study Tools.

3. *Journal what you learn*—If you are anything like me, then your memory is not what it was when you were a kid. I frequently forget where I put my keys or my cell phone. If that is the case with my keys or my phone, I can only imagine how little I retain

from my time studying the Bible. That is why I started writing down what I have learned in notebooks every time I sit down to study. Sometimes I only write one or two sentences. Other days, I write one or two pages. This habit allows me to look back at what I have learned from day to day. I also start a new notebook for each book of the Bible I read, which has become a great resource for me when I preach or have a question about a passage I have studied.

PRAY OVER WHAT YOU READ/STUDY

We can be diligent in the reading and study of Scripture, but this divinely inspired book should never be treated as just an academic work. The Bible is the living, active, breathed-out Word of God to those who call on His name. It is written by the hand of God through the actual hands of the people who penned the letters. With that sort of divine power contained in its words, our efforts alone will never be able to fully grasp its weight. That is why Paul prays for the church at Ephesus in Ephesians 1:16–18: "I do not cease to give thanks for you, remembering you in my prayers, that the God of our Lord Jesus Christ, the Father of glory, may give you the Spirit of wisdom and of revelation in the knowledge of him, having the eyes of your hearts enlightened, that you may know what is the hope to which he has called you, what are the riches of his glorious inheritance in the saints."

May we as His people constantly find ourselves asking for God's grace and wisdom as we search the breadth of His Word to know Him fully. God, help us to grasp your beauty, your power, and your truth as we seek to be children of God who look more and more like your Son every day.

MEDITATE ON IT

As much as we read, study, and journal the verses that we have
learned throughout the Bible, we also must revisit the Word
time and time again. There is great value in reading and writing the Word of God, but there is also a richness in writing the
Word on our hearts. The person who has the powerful Word
of God stored away in her heart, ready to use at any moment,
is a person that truly is blessed. As the psalmist says:

> Blessed is the man
>   who walks not in the counsel of the wicked,
> nor stands in the way of sinners,
>   nor sits in the seat of scoffers;
> but his delight is in the law of the LORD,
>   and on his law he meditates day and night.
>   (Psalm 1:1–2)

The Hebrew word for "meditates" literally means "mutters"
or "speaks." The person who walks in the counsel of the Lord
speaks the Word of the Lord to himself consistently. I cannot
read, write, or listen to Scripture all day every day, so how can
I meditate on it day and night? By memorizing and meditating
on Scripture, I can delight in God's Word at any moment and
follow His commands: "I have stored up your word in my heart,
that I might not sin against you" (Psalm 119:11).

Again, many of us do not have the memory that we once
did, but that does not have to stop us from trying to memorize
Scripture. One of the most effective tactics that I have found
for memorizing Scripture is to write the same verse on four or
five sticky notes. Then I stick them all around the house. I will
put a note on my steering wheel (which is a great road rage
deterrent); I will put a note on my laptop display; or I will put
a note on the back of my iPhone. There are plenty of weeks

where I will write a verse on my bathroom mirror with a dry-erase marker. I try to do whatever I can to flood my everyday steps with the Word of God.

These reminders around me have proven extremely useful for hiding God's Word in my heart where it has been both a comfort to me and others in their time of need. I have been able to use those Scriptures in conversations with friends and family in their time of need. I have quoted Scripture in sermons on the fly where the Holy Spirit brought it out from the storehouse of my heart to be used while I preached.

We meditate knowing that the Word of God is never ineffective. It always molds and shapes us to the will of God and equips us for the purpose of God. It does not lose its efficacy, even if it quietly sits in the heart of the believer. We meditate and memorize knowing that Scripture will accomplish many great things in our lives, even if it is for a day yet to come.

TALK ABOUT IT

I have spent the vast majority of my life in the middle of the Bible Belt. Living in this area and being a pastor here for years, I have seen some assumptions of believers in the church in the South. These assumptions can create some dangerous behaviors in the lives of Christians. One assumption is: everyone believes what I believe, and everyone has heard the gospel that I have heard. This creates a passivity in the spiritual lives of many. The gospel in the South is something to be consumed and not necessarily shared because everyone already knows it.

The assumption of widespread belief and the passivity that follows foster a Christian silence in many churches today. It leads to a rhythm where we ingest the Word of God through a Sunday sermon and we do not revisit the Scripture until seven days later at the same time and the same place. Scripture is

meant to be vocalized and not just in the mutterings of medi-
ation. We ought to speak Scripture over the people that God
has sovereignly placed in our lives. We should speak it over
our coworkers, our church friends, our lost friends, and especially our family.

Talking about the Scriptures inside our own homes is one
of the primary means for us to grow in our faith. That is why
God is so direct when He commands Israel in Deuteronomy
6:6–7: "And these words that I command you today shall be
on your heart. You shall teach them diligently to your children, and shall talk of them when you sit in your house, and
when you walk by the way, and when you lie down, and when
you rise."

God means for you to grow in grace by sharing what you
are learning about God with the people you love the most. This
can come through dedicated time where you read Scripture as
a family. This can come from when you talk about what you
learned at church when you are driving home after Sunday service. It can happen when a casual conversation takes a decidedly Christ-oriented tone.

We do not have to be with our blood relatives for this to
happen. It can happen with anyone, anywhere, at any given
time, and all we have to do is to store up Scripture in our heart
and then talk about it when the time presents itself. When we
expect it or when we are totally surprised, let us not waste an
opportunity to talk about the God we serve by using His very
words to do it.

TURN TO THE BIBLE IN HARD TIMES

The pain and trials of our lives have an ability to isolate and
insulate us from the things that matter to us the most. I often
hear people say in the midst of hardship: "It feels like God is

not there." When darkness envelops us and all we can feel is the dull, constant groaning of this world, it can seem like all that is good has disappeared.

Our struggles in the present and the fear of what may come have the ability to choke out the light of the promises of God. Those promises remain. They have not gone anywhere or left our spiritual lives for reasons beyond our control. Our issue is something is obscuring our view of those promises. It may be darkness; it may be spiritual attack; it may be our emotions; or it may be the valley that we are in.

As Christians, we have to find ways to peer through the darkness or look around life's obstacles so we can see the promises of God for us. I cannot help but think of Joshua as I reflect on a wave of hurt and fear crashing into someone's life. Moses goes to be in the presence of the Lord at the end of the book of Deuteronomy, placing Joshua as the leader of the nation of Israel. Not only does Joshua have to take on the mantle of leadership, but he does so knowing that he has to replace one of the most prominent men of faith of his day.

I am sure there was plenty of grumbling directed toward Joshua in the early days of his leadership. There were new pressures and his to-do list was never complete. Wars were being laid out and fought. The promised land was still just that—a promise. There was plenty in the early days of Joshua's leadership that would obstruct his view of the promises of God.

God wanted to be sure that Joshua stayed focused on the One who had called him for this time and role. He reminded Joshua in Joshua 1:8–9: "This Book of the Law shall not depart from your mouth, but you shall meditate on it day and night, so that you may be careful to do according to all that is written in it. For then you will make your way prosperous, and then you will have good success. Have I not commanded you? Be strong and courageous. Do not be frightened, and do not be dismayed, for the LORD your God is with you wherever you go."

The call for Joshua to be strong and courageous was tied directly to meditating on the book of the law. God's laws and ordinances were God's promise to the people of Israel. Joshua was to lead the people according to God's law, and he had the promise that those laws were given to the people of God as a sign of God's faithfulness to carry them by His strength. Joshua would only be able to navigate the mountains and valleys that lay ahead by turning to the Word of the Lord day in and day out.

So it is for us—God's Word is His promise to us. He is with us, He loves us, He will not forsake us, and He is working in us. Those promises can be quickly forgotten on the roller coaster of life. Despite our feelings and our fears, we must turn to His Word in the darkest of days, knowing the One who promised He is with us is faithful. May we remind ourselves of that faithful presence even when our fears tell us otherwise.

His Word is a great gift to the church and to the people of God. It is a way by which we grow, we love, and we withstand the brokenness of this world. May we seek His Word in our days and in our homes. May we study, speak, and soak in the power of His promises.

CHAPTER 4

HONORING GOD IN EVERY STEP

So teach us to number our days
that we may get a heart of wisdom.
PSALM 90:12

In February 2019, I was sitting on the back porch of my home. I was gearing up to do some sermon prep but had stepped outside to get some fresh air before I began the hours of long work with a notepad and a pile of commentaries. As I soaked in the last few rays of sunshine, a Twitter notification popped up on my phone: *VA Governor Talks About Late-Term Abortion.*

Interested, I clicked the link that took me to a radio interview that Governor Ralph Northam had just given on abortion legislation that was moving through the Virginia legislature at the time. In the bill was the justification for late-term abortion if there was a disability or abnormality. Then Governor Northam described a provisional conversation that could go on between doctor and mother thanks to this new bill.

According to Northam, "An infant would be delivered, the infant would be kept comfortable, then the infant would be resuscitated—if that's what the mother and the family desired—and then a discussion would ensue between the physicians and the mother."⁴ That conversation between physician and mother would be to decide whether a newly born baby should live or die.

I was shaken to my very core. Not only is such a conversation heartbreaking, but that conversation was had over my life in the seconds after I was born. When I was born, I was not breathing or moving, and the doctor said nothing apart from one simple question:

"Do you want us to let him go?"

Those were the words that welcomed me into the world as that doctor held my armless and lifeless body in his arms. As he assessed me and my situation, he told my parents that I was "not viable." His best-case scenario was even if I could somehow survive, I would never lead a "full life."

I thank God that my parents did not hesitate at what the doctor said. "Do whatever you can to revive him" was their simple but strong reply, and by God's grace I lived. And by God's grace, the medical prophecies of my unviability and my inability to lead a full life unraveled quickly. I look across the landscape of my life and see a whole lot that looks like a "full life."

After listening to the interview, my thoughts went immediately to moms all across Virginia who would come face to face with this high-pressure decision and conversation. I thought of how this legislation was devaluing the lives of children with all sorts of disabilities. This bill was set to mark kids like me as disposable and not worthy of life. I had to do something. I had to speak out against this awful bill.

I shot a quick video where I spoke to the value of life and the value of disabled lives like mine. I spoke against the devaluing of human life that this Virginia legislation was looking to enact. I took that video and posted it to Twitter.

In a matter of hours, the video had been shared and viewed thousands of times. I was receiving all sorts of feedback on social media—some encouraging and some bombastic. I also received a slew of emails in the days following the video. One of those emails was from a staffer at Fox News: "Can you turn your video into an 800-word op-ed? We want to run it this weekend."

Obviously, I was surprised that my short video had caught anyone's attention, much less a national news organization. I put off my sermon prep for a couple of hours and crafted a short opinion piece of why my life and disabled lives have meaning and value. I finished the piece and sent it off the same day I had shot the video.

The piece went live on the Fox News website on Saturday, and it went about as well as you would expect for an opinion piece on abortion. There was lots of positive feedback, but there were also social media trolls who attacked me, my faith, my wife, and my family. Almost overnight I had made my family a target for the Internet to lash out at. This was not going like I had planned.

I went to bed early that night because I had to wake early the next morning to go and preach at a church in South Carolina. The next morning was a beautiful time of worship with some really sweet people. After finishing my sermon, I hopped back into my car to head back home. I pulled my phone out so I could use navigation to get me back on the interstate. As my home screen lit up, there was a lone email notification. It was another email from a Fox News staffer.

"Hey Daniel, I work for a Fox News show called *The Story with Martha MacCallum* and we wanted you to know that we loved your article. We would love if you could come on the show and talk about it. Can you be in New York City tomorrow night?"

Again, I was absolutely stunned. I never saw myself going on any sort of show like that, but I also wondered if I should in the first place. I am not an overly political guy. I am a Christ-first, Christ-as-King kind of guy. I did not want people to see me as a political chess piece more than an image-bearer of God. I needed to go home and bounce ideas off my wife. After a long and weighty discussion, I decided to go ahead with the interview.

I flew to New York City that next morning, all the while emailing with show staff going over what we would touch on during the course of my interview. We knew we would talk about my reaction to Governor Northam's comments, my birth story, and the value of babies with disabilities. I spent all my attention that day crafting clear and concise answers for each question.

Come that night, everything went flawlessly according to their minute-by-minute plan. Finally, I headed into the studio to do my interview with Martha. The interview was going just like they said it would, until Martha asked me a question I had not prepared for: "Something happened when you were fifteen years old that changed your life. What was it?"

My mind raced for a split second as I tried to figure out how my teenage years tied into the pro-life ethic. Then I realized it did not. Martha did not want me to share about abortion legislation in that moment, she wanted me to share about the Giver of life. For the next thirty seconds, I shared the gospel with the 4.5 million people watching that night.

In that moment, it all made sense. Just seven days before, I'd had my day planned out, and it mostly involved sunshine and sermons. Yet, things unfolded in ways I could have never foreseen. One moment of sharing a video to social media created a cascade of events that allowed me to share the gospel with more people than I will likely ever speak to during my ministry lifetime.

In an instant my life changed, just as it has in so many other moments of my life. Some of those moments—like the first time I met my wife—were moments of awe-inspiring grace. Other sudden moments—like when my dad was diagnosed with cancer—shook me to the core.

Enduring means that sooner or later life will unfold in ways that we cannot see coming. One of the most difficult aspects of navigating the unforeseen is when everything falls apart. Our job status, our health, family dynamics, and the call of God can all change in one sweeping wave. How do we trust that our circumstances fall into "all things" that work together for good? How can I move forward when all my plans are shattered by unforeseen circumstances?

While we cannot know the future, we can live in such a way that allows us to navigate the mountains and the valleys of life. We can set up rhythms now that will help us stand when our world changes in the blink of an eye. Here are some rhythms we can invest in now that can help us when sudden changes come.

DREAM AND PLAN FOR THE FUTURE IN BIG WAYS

What was the worst purchase of 2020? A daily planner.

Jokes aside, 2020 was a year that was hard for those who had plans for their personal life, family life, business, or the life of their church. Aside from the first three months of the year, most of the plans people had hoped for fell by the wayside as the pandemic swept in. The age of self-isolation shut down most of people's plans at best and at worst put them in a massive hole to start 2021. Where did that leave believers as they began to plan and dream for what may lay ahead?

Hopeful.

We do not look back and grieve over hard years as people who do not have hope. We are people who know the faithful One to whom we trust our lives, and He is not going to leave our sides regardless of what may come our way in the near or distant future. He holds our lives in His sovereign hands, and He will redeem hard seasons and painful years.

As we look back, we can remain hopeful. As we look to the future, we do not have to feel presumptuous about planning ahead. The Lord controls all things, and we will not boast about what lies ahead, but we can make plans with open hands, knowing that the Lord may lead us elsewhere.

Planning out my year and setting goals was a weakness of mine for many years. I liked to roll with life's punches with no real plan in mind. That was true even of my preaching. I would sit down at my desk a week out from preaching and try to figure out what sermon to prepare for our people.

That all changed about eight years ago when another pastor friend told me about how he would exposit books of the Bible for his church. He would sit down and plan out the next few months' worth of sermon text. He would pick the Scriptures, write down a few main themes, and assign each Scripture a Sunday. That way, he knew what his sermon text was for each week without having to come up with a catchy theme or title. He just preached what the Scripture laid out.

That conversation led me to start doing sermon series through books of the Bible by planning them months in advance, but it also started me down a path of planning more things in all corners of my life. I began to meet with my wife every January to talk through what worked and what didn't in the previous year. We talk about how we can grow in the next year and how to plan accordingly. This ranges from goals within the ministry to goals in our marriage to what we want to save for or how many dates to plan.

Your plans and your goals are going to look so much different than mine. They could be long-term or short-term, but assess what is going on in your life and make plans about how you can grow. Some plans may never come to fruition because of unforeseen circumstances, but that should not prevent us from trying to make the most of our days, as we see in Proverbs 6:6–8:

> Go to the ant, O sluggard;
>> consider her ways, and be wise.
> Without having any chief,
>> officer, or ruler,
> she prepares her bread in summer
>> and gathers her food in harvest.
> How long will you lie there, O sluggard?
>> When will you arise from your sleep?

Scripture reminds us of the life of the ant. Here is a little creature with a little life span. It works hard in the summer to store up food for the winter. It is a winter that the ant may never see, but it works nonetheless for what may come. So we must do the same in working and preparing for what may come. Plan, hope, and dream for the days to come. Seek to make the most of each day that God has granted you, knowing that one day you will give an account for each day lived.

DO NOT QUIT WHEN CHANGE COMES

Knowing both the omniscient nature of God and the limitations of people, there is one guarantee when it comes to the plans of humanity: they will fail. We might have thought of all the possible outcomes and contingencies, but our plans will eventually unravel. Circumstances happen that are out of our control.

We must come to grips with the fact that we simply do not know the future. As Proverbs 20:24 plainly declares, "A man's steps are from the LORD; how then can man understand his way?" We are not the sole writer of our story. As much as we want to be self-sovereign, it is God who lays out the story before us. So what do we do when our story has a plot twist? We try our best to adapt and trust God as we do.

Many of us will admit that change is an incredibly hard thing to walk through. We are all creatures of habit and having to navigate new surroundings can be distressing. I think that is one of the reasons why so many of us bristled at the phrase "new normal" during the COVID-19 quarantine. Some of our resistance to the "new normal" was that things that should not be normalized (limited human interaction or virtual church) were being referred to as normal. Some changes (like wearing masks and social distancing) were not comfortable.

Change on the microscale is uncomfortable; change on the macroscale can be devastating. When trials come and devastate the landscape of my life, how can I move forward? How can I pivot into a "new normal" when I have no idea what I am doing?

Persevere.

God has made you and saved you for more than succumbing to your circumstances. In fact, God uses the trials and the sudden changes in our lives to peel away the layers of our self-sufficiency while revealing more of His present strength in our lives. He is calling us to endure and press forward even in the darkness of the unknown. The scriptural call to press on and endure is robust:

> Not only that, but we rejoice in our sufferings, knowing that suffering produces endurance, and endurance produces character, and character produces hope. (Romans 5:3–4)

Count it all joy, my brothers, when you meet trials of various kinds, for you know that the testing of your faith produces steadfastness. (James 1:2–3)

Therefore do not throw away your confidence, which has a great reward. For you have need of endurance, so that when you have done the will of God you may receive what is promised. (Hebrews 10:35–36)

Rejoice in hope, be patient in tribulation, be constant in prayer. (Romans 12:12)

This is not meant to be some sort of hyper-motivational "don't quit on you" part of the book. This is a call not to quit on the plans that God has for your life in the midst of trials and change. There is a biblical promise that you will face hardship in this life. There is no doubt that your ideal life scenarios will not go the way you wanted. When that happens—when the world stops on a dime—do not quit. God has a plan for you that extends far beyond walking away.

LAMENT WHAT IS LOST

While it is paramount for believers to endure amid hardship, it is also unhealthy to ignore the pain that envelops us. One coping technique people have is to act like nothing is wrong while the world burns down around them. That behavior is seen just as much inside the church as outside of the church. We experience loss and hurt, but we convince ourselves and others that everything is OK—but it is not.

It is healthy for us to grieve what we have lost and to lament the hardships of this life, but so many of us do not do that. Many of us think there is no room for that in the life of the believer. My friend Mason King once said, "The modern evangelical church has lost the language of lament, forgetting that almost one-third of the Psalms are laments. God not only gives us permission to be sad and to want things to change, He gives us a language for it."

Mason's words ring true in a Christian culture that feels the pressure to be perceived as perfect, even as the laments of Psalms echo in the background of our faith.

> How long, O LORD? Will you forget me forever?
>   How long will you hide your face from me?
> How long must I take counsel in my soul
>   and have sorrow in my heart all the day?
> How long shall my enemy be exalted over me?
>
> Consider and answer me, O LORD my God;
>   light up my eyes, lest I sleep the sleep of death,
> lest my enemy say, "I have prevailed over him,"
>   lest my foes rejoice because I am shaken.
>
> But I have trusted in your steadfast love;
>   my heart shall rejoice in your salvation.
> I will sing to the LORD,
>   because he has dealt bountifully with me. (Psalm 13)

God has given us the language to mourn and grieve over what we lost in trial or change. He can handle our heartache. He wants to hear the cries of your heart, and He will mourn with you. Take your hurt to the Lord. Tell Him about your grief over what you have lost or what has changed in your life.

Take your hurt to others and weep together. Meaningful community cannot be forged if we are not willing to share all the parts of who we are—good or bad. Cry out, grieve, and lament. The way we move forward is to address what we have lost.

PLAN WITH GOD'S GLORY IN MIND

Trust in the LORD with all your heart,
and do not lean on your own understanding.
In all your ways acknowledge him,
and he will make straight your paths.
PROVERBS 3:5-6

Many of the plans and dreams we have are world focused, but how can we plan our days and years to be focused on the glory of God? One of the places to start is being intentional about it. We need to take a long look at our life and make an effort to leverage every opportunity to display the glory of God in all the world.

I trust God with a lot in my everyday life. I trust Him with my salvation, my sanctification, my purpose, my comings and goings, and even my very existence. Some of that trust is conscious, while at other times I forget the work of God in my life.

Just as I can overlook the parts of my life that I have trusted to the Lord, I can easily overlook the opportunities I have to acknowledge Him in the things that I do. Our worship and acknowledgement of Him can take all sorts of forms, but one of the most basic ways that I can make plans by acknowledging Him is to regularly be a part of a church. This does not happen by accident. Showing up on Sunday morning is often a Saturday night decision. Make choices that free you up to be a part of a church or to even serve regularly at your church.

Make decisions and plans that allow you to glorify God with your means. Budget your tithes. Give baby supplies to a local pregnancy center. Ask missionaries how you can support them beyond just a monthly gift. Taking time to assess our material possessions allows us the freedom to be generous with what we have. Christian generosity flows from the person who is intentional about giving to the watching world—all for the glory of God.

MAKE ROOM FOR SOVEREIGN APPOINTMENTS

Just as we should steward our calendars and our means, so we should steward the divine appointments that God puts in our way. What do I mean when I say "divine appointments"? These are the unexpected moments we have to encourage a person who is having a tough week. It is the time that a chance encounter at a grocery store turns into a conversation about the gospel. They are the moments that every Great-Commission-focused Christian hopes for but can never anticipate.

Yet, how many of these moments get thrown away because our lives are too busy or our attention is captivated by our devices? In my own life, I have had far too many times where I had to say, "I would love to stay and talk but I've got to go." I have had far too many gospel opportunities slip away because I have had to hurry off to the next thing on my to-do list.

Going back ten years ago, these "too busy" moments were happening frequently. I was a youth pastor, and I was working with a high school football team, as well as providing leadership in two different community organizations. I was always running from one thing to the next with little wiggle room in between.

In that time, there were countless "divine appointments" that I was having to hurry past. These moments in my life are quite frequent. Many times when I stop to eat at a fast food restaurant or stop at the gas station, I capture people's attention. That is totally understandable because I know many people do not regularly see someone eat a cheeseburger with their toes or put gas in the car with their feet. These moments of natural curiosity quickly turn to people asking me about my armless situation and eventually how I came to deal with my armlessness. It is a ready-made gospel conversation.

I made a conscious decision years ago to budget a little extra time for every errand, every meal on the go, and every trip I take to the grocery store. That little margin affords me more opportunities to share the hope I have in Christ with people who are genuinely willing to listen. Our opportunities to share gospel hope and love with people are rarely ever anticipated in our everyday lives, so we have to make the effort to give space for those divine appointments to breathe.

Imagine if the good Samaritan in Luke 10 was too busy with his journey to notice or take time for the beaten man. Imagine if he had not saved those two days' worth of wages to pay for the man's care at an inn. The Samaritan created the margin in his life to love the beaten man well. He had decided in his heart to live out what God had commanded by making space in his life.

Our margins are going to look different from person to person. Some of us need to make space in our week to be present in the lives of our friends. Some of us need to plan margins in our budget so that we can meet the needs of a person in our church. Some of us simply need margins in our daily schedule to sit and talk with our kids about what is happening in their lives. We rarely see divine appointments coming, but may we live in such a way that allows us to make the most of them when they appear.

God can take just a moment and use it in reverberating ways for His glory. We simply must live our lives in a way that honors Him in every step and bump along the way. Life will not always go according to *our* plans, but we can endure the trials that come so that we can grow in Christ and go on mission. There will be plenty of twists and turns along our journey, but let us embrace what we are in the middle of right now so that we can race with endurance.

CHAPTER 5

PRAYER

First of all, then, I urge that supplications, prayers, intercessions,
and thanksgivings be made for all people.
1 TIMOTHY 2:1

The days following my salvation were definitely days of growth in my faith. I was just beginning to scratch the surface of what it means to follow Jesus. My mom had just started laying out what studying Scripture looks like and why it is such an important part of my spiritual life. My youth pastor was showing me why people who follow Jesus serve and love those who do not know Him.

There were many lessons being laid out for me intellectually, and it was a season of growth. Little did I know that my growth was about to take another step forward, but this time it would not be because of a lesson taught by a parent or in a youth group. God was about to cement my understanding of prayer and faith through the circumstances of the next few months.

Other than being born without arms, I was a healthy kid growing up. I never really got sick and did not have any known health issues. That all changed when I was thirteen years old.

I had gone to my local family doctor to get a routine physical so I could play sports that fall. As the doctor looked me over, he noticed my spine had a slight curvature to it. He thought I may have scoliosis, which is a somewhat common curving of the spine and is most prevalent during adolescence. There was nothing to be concerned about at that time, but my doctors wanted to keep an eye on it over the next few years.

As I turned fifteen, I hit the biggest growth spurt of my entire life. In just ten months I grew five inches and put on twenty-five pounds. I had the typical growing pains, but I also noticed some stiffness in my back that my normally flexible body was not used to. My parents and I were worried that my scoliosis was progressing to the point of being a health concern.

A month later, a doctor at Duke Children's Hospital confirmed our fears. My scoliosis had worsened significantly in just twelve months. What was once a slight curvature in my spine was now significant. I will never forget looking at the X-ray with my doctor that day and seeing two large curves that had twisted my spine into an "S." With such a drastic change in the structure of my spine, the doctors wanted to see me in thirty days so they could monitor the curvature closely.

At the appointment thirty days later, my situation had only gotten worse. The doctors were deeply concerned about my long-term health, knowing that severe cases of scoliosis can cause damage to the spine, hips, and legs if steps are not taken to correct the curvature. There were only two options. The first was to wear a body brace, which would hold the spine in place and stop the progression of the curves. The second option was spinal fusion surgery, where doctors would permanently straighten my spine by fusing two titanium rods to the spine. Doctors set up one more appointment thirty days out. If things had not improved in my spine, we would decide on a course of treatment.

Both treatment options would be devastating to my everyday life. I bend my spine in harsh ways to accomplish everyday tasks with my feet. Both a brace and surgery would prevent me from bending my body like I needed to. Either option would force me to relearn how to do every single thing in my life. I needed a literal miracle or my life was going to change significantly in just a month. I needed God to step into my life in a massive way, and I needed Him to do it soon.

The only thing in my power that I could do was pray, but even at that early stage in my faith, I knew that God may not answer my prayers in the way I would prefer. I realized that I may not be healed, but I also knew the God I had given my life to. He was the Maker of the heavens and the earth. He made lame people walk and blind people see. He called my spiritually dead body to life through the power of the gospel. His power and might could heal my twisting spine, but was it His will to heal me?

It was so hard to pray to God through all of my fear, worry, and doubt by asking Him, "Not my will but Your will be done." God was already using my armlessness for His glory and purposes, so it was not a wild thing to think that God could use the struggle of surgery to allow the world to know more about Him. The night before my final appointment my parents and I huddled together to pray on our living room floor. I remember my mom praying, "God, please heal Daniel, but even if You don't, I pray You use Daniel for Your glory even in his pain."

The next morning, I walked into Duke Children's Hospital very slowly as fear after fear poured through my mind. As my dad and I sat in the waiting room, I prayed quietly to myself,

"Not my will, Your will. ... Not my will, Your will." The next hour or so went by in a blur. I went back for X-rays and then waited for a while until a nurse came and pulled me back for a second set of X-rays, which I had never done for any of my previous visits. We got done with those and I was sent to an exam room.

I will never forget my doctor coming into the room without a word and walking over to a backlit display to hang my X-ray. "I simply cannot believe what I am seeing," he said. "That is why I had you do two X-rays. Curves like this just do not improve."

God had healed me.

No surgery. No brace. I could live my life like I had become accustomed to—all by His grace. I honestly do not know how I would have reacted if the diagnosis had been a grave one, but I do know that God was changing my heart in those thirty days. I became more apt to go to God in prayer about anything in my life. I prayed to Him about my health concerns but also about all my other joys, hurts, and fears. I sought His will in my life more regularly. God was changing everything about me because I was spending time with Him.

Even deeper than my trust in God was my growth in the belief of the power of prayer. God may not desire for all our prayers to be answered, but when we petition God for the things in our lives we desire to see happen, the planet can be altered by prayer. Jesus tells us of the power of prayer in Mark 11:23–24: "Truly, I say to you, whoever says to this mountain, 'Be taken up and thrown into the sea,' and does not doubt in his heart, but believes that what he says will come to pass, it will be done for him. Therefore I tell you, whatever you ask in prayer, believe that you have received it, and it will be yours."

Prayer has tremendous power for the believer, but I often allow my miniature attention span to stand between me and a consistent prayer life. I struggle at times to know how to pray and what to pray, but God has been faithful in teaching me through those times what a functioning prayer life can look like on an ongoing basis. Let us take a look at rhythms we can walk in to help us pray our way through the days as we live out our faith with endurance.

PRAY FOR THE MISSION OF GOD

One thing is apparent in American culture: the level of lostness. The culture at large does not value, much less is aware of, Jesus and His gospel. It does not take very long for a person to observe that the United States is a post-Christian nation. It is not just that the culture has distanced itself from biblical morals; it has distanced itself from the God of the Bible altogether.

That is just a snapshot of how many people do not know Jesus in my little bubble of the world. To cast our vision globally, it is even more heartbreaking to know that there are nearly 3.23 billion people on the planet that have never heard of the gospel and have no access to it.[5] Just under half of the population does not have the hope of Jesus.

Then there are the people closest to us: our family, our friends, our coworkers, and our classmates. How many of them do not know Jesus as Lord? They have nowhere to turn for their hope and their salvation apart from their own efforts, which will inevitably send them to an eternity separated from Jesus. Those we see on a daily basis need Jesus as their Lord just as much as people on the other side of the planet whom we will never see.

The need for salvation is great in our towns, in our country, and in our world. God knows the need, and it is one of the reasons why Jesus, in the moments before His ascension, sent all of His disciples into all the corners of the world to make more disciples. God's mission for those who follow Him is that we would teach everyone about the One who saved us and then send them to do the same.

This is why we pray for the mission of God to be done in this world. We can pray as Paul asked the church at Thessalonica to pray, "Finally, brothers, pray for us, that the word of the Lord may speed ahead and be honored, as happened among you" (2 Thessalonians 3:1). Just as we came to know Jesus as Lord, may the world come to know Jesus through the willingness and efforts of His church to go on mission. We pray for indigenous churches, for more missionaries, and for the seed of the gospel to fall on fertile hearts. We pray that the gospel of God will spread through every people and country and tribe—all for the glory of God.

PRAY FOR THE PEOPLE OF GOD

If you are reading this book, there is a strong likelihood that you are in some sort of faith community. Maybe you are a part of a local church that loves you, leads you, and is helping you grow in Christ. Maybe someone who loves you gave you this book in the hopes that you would endure in your faith with Jesus as Lord. On some level, there are people in your life that love Jesus and that love you.

Pray for them. Pray that they would love Jesus more today than they did yesterday. Pray that they would stand strong through the trials and temptations they are certain to face in the coming days. Pray that God would use them in the lives of others, just like He used them in your life. Pray that they would be united with other believers, as Jesus prayed to the Father: "I do not ask for these only, but also for those who will believe in me through their word, that they may all be one, just as you, Father, are in me, and I in you, that they also may be in us, so that the world may believe that you have sent me" (John 17:20–21).

As fellow Christians, we can identify with the needs and struggles of those that God has put in our lives. He has given us a community of believers who can support one another through prayer in times of need. I know there are many times I have come across a friend who was going through a difficult time and I have offered up the phrase, "I will definitely pray for you." It almost goes without saying that I have forgotten to pray for a person in particular on many occasions. One of the things I started doing to combat my forgetfulness was to pray for that person as soon as the need was made known. It was awkward the first few times I prayed in the church parking lot or at a grocery store, but it allowed me to pray for my friend as well as give them the reminder that they are not alone in what they have to go through in this life. One of the most encouraging things we can do is to pray over the people we love face to face.

I will never forget being a teenager and having my youth pastor's wife pray over me. Her name is Dee Hall and she is now, and was then, a praying woman. I struggled with insecurity in my late teens because I feared I would never get married. I assumed that there was not a single woman on the planet who would want to marry a man like me. Dee knew those fears that I had, and one day as I was leaving church, she asked if she could pray for me. Right there, on the sidewalk in front of our church, she prayed for me. She prayed for my future wife, my future kids, and my future ministry. It was one of the most encouraging moments of my life.

Dee did not need to write a note or give me a gift so that I could be encouraged. She saw the fears waging war in my heart, and she brought those fears to God on my behalf. She understood the need of the hour and took it to the One who could do something about it. She loved me in a way that only a sister in Christ could: she asked our Father for help.

PRAY FOR THE CHURCH OF GOD

Scripture tells us not even the gates of hell will prevail against the church of God (Matthew 16:18), but that will not stop Satan from trying. Even though the defeat of Satan is promised in Revelation, he is determined to attack the work of God in any way that he can, and one of the tools he uses is division. From both within the church and without, Satan puts us under all sorts of divisive attacks.

Jesus knew that Satan would try to scatter His church through division and that is why He prayed for unity in John 17. The unity of the church of God is a living, breathing illustration that the church is brought together by means that could not possibly be human. The church being united underneath the work of Christ is vital for the spread of the gospel. That is why we must be vigilant in praying for the church.

The apostle Paul prayed for the church constantly. Many of the epistles that he wrote in the New Testament start off with a prayer for a specific church. He never ceased praying for the church of God (Colossians 1:9).

There are so many ways to pray for the church. We can pray for the elders of our church and that God would be the primary focus in their lives and leadership. We can pray that our church would be faithful to and focused on reaching the community that God has sovereignly placed them in with the gospel. We can pray that we would see our fellow church members as family—brothers and sisters in Christ—and not as the sum of their votes or preferences.

It is difficult to be divided as a church when its members are unceasing in their prayers for one another. The church needs the grace of God to be united for the mission of God. Let us be faithful to pray to that end so that the work of God may be seen in how His church moves together with one single purpose and pursuit.

PRAY AS A MEANS OF WORSHIP

There are many times we go to God in prayer as a way of asking Him for something, but prayer does not have to be confined to requests. Prayer can be an expression of thanks for what we have received by the gracious hand of God. It can be adoration and worship of our God.

Paul models this in Colossians 1:12–14 as he is "giving thanks to the Father, who has qualified you to share in the inheritance of the saints in light. He has delivered us from the domain of darkness and transferred us to the kingdom of his beloved Son, in whom we have redemption, the forgiveness of sins." This Pauline prayer shows us that the Christian can use prayer as a means of worship.

For many of us, worship happens in a Sunday church service through a hymn or a worship song, but worship was never meant to be isolated to one hour of our week. Worship is not merely singing. Worship is the use of our entire lives. That is a truly acceptable form of worship (Romans 12:1).

Take time to pray without asking God for a thing. Pray and worship God for all the kindness He has showered you with in your daily life. Thank God for waking up, for your loved ones, for the fruit of the Spirit in your life, or even for the beauty of creation that you get to see and hear every day. Worship God in prayer by praising His love, His justice, His power, and His mercy. Let us use our prayer lives to worship the One who is listening to the cries and meditations of our hearts.

PRAY SCRIPTURE

Many times I feel like I do not have the adequate words to express what is going on in my heart and my head. I struggle to capture the weight of my hurt or the majesty of the character of God. My words are limited, but His words never are. His Word carries a power and a Holy-Spirit-wrought purpose that my words never will. That is why there is beauty in using Scripture in our prayers to God.

In God's Word, we see a strong tie between praying in the Spirit and using the sword of the Spirit (Scripture). As we are exhorted in Ephesians 6 to put on the whole armor of God for withstanding the work of Satan, we see how interwoven Scripture and prayer really are. Ephesians 6:17–18 says, "Take the helmet of salvation, and the sword of the Spirit, which is the word of God, praying at all times in the Spirit, with all prayer and supplication. To that end, keep alert with all perseverance, making supplication for all the saints."

One of the ways we can stay in step with the Spirit as we pray is to use the very words that the Holy Spirit penned in our prayers back to Him. I will never capture the grandeur of God like Isaiah did when he got a glimpse of the throne room of heaven in Isaiah 6. My worship of who God is will only be strengthened by the praise of the faithfulness of God in Psalm 57. There are times when there is no other way to put my sadness and brokenness into words like David did in Psalm 6.

Scripture is a lamp to our feet and a light to our path—especially in our prayers. It shines in ways that the words of people never can. Find some of those beautiful and powerful passages of Scripture. Find ways to sew them into your prayers or even just use Bible passages as your entire prayer. Scripture is not just a way to mold our hearts, but it is also a way to express our hearts to God when our own words are not enough.

PRAY EVEN WHEN YOU DO
NOT KNOW WHAT TO SAY

There are many times in our lives when we feel overwhelmed by fear and the gravity of the circumstances we are up against. Our minds are clouded by our sadness and hurt. We simply do not have the head space or energy to put coherent thoughts together, even when we need the Father to carry the burden that has quickly entangled us.

There have been many times when I have not prayed because I did not feel like I had the words to adequately express my heart to God. Yet, as Scripture teaches us, God is so incredibly kind that He helps us even in the times when we cannot ask: "The Spirit helps us in our weakness. For we do not know what to pray for as we ought, but the Spirit himself intercedes for us with groanings too deep for words. And he who searches hearts knows what is the mind of the Spirit, because the Spirit intercedes for the saints according to the will of God" (Romans 8:26–27).

The Holy Spirit is placed in the life of the believer the moment they are saved (Ephesians 1:13). The Spirit is the promise of what is to come once we pass from this life into eternity, but He is also so much more. Scripture describes Him as both an advocate and a friend to those in Christ. When Jesus told of the coming of the Holy Spirit to His disciples, He said, "It is to your advantage that I go away, for if I do not go away, the Helper will not come to you" (John 16:7).

Isn't it amazing that Jesus told His disciples it was better for Him to go so the Holy Spirit could be in them? While Jesus was doing many amazing works before the disciples, the Helper was coming to do many amazing things in the disciples. The Spirit cultivates the spiritual fruit in our lives so that both the watching world and our own hearts may be encouraged. He prompts the hearts of people to serve and go in ways they would never think to do.

The Holy Spirit also supports us in our prayer life when the words have escaped us. When believers do not have the faintest idea of what to say, the Spirit is active in their hearts. He knows everything about us: our hearts, our hurts, and our feelings. He takes all of that and expresses what is going on in us to the Father. Even when our words fail us in prayer, the Spirit will not. In those wordless days and seasons, be still before God, and the Spirit will do what your words cannot.

PRAY FOR THE STRENGTH TO STAND

I do not think I am going out on a limb when I say that life is hard. Many things we have to face are difficult: our jobs, parenting, marriage, maintaining friendships, fighting fear, navigating hardship, and loving hard-to-love people. Those are hard enough to withstand in isolation, much less when you have to deal with a number of difficulties all at once.

God understands how difficult it is to be human. He sympathizes with us in our weakness, but He also promised that life would be filled with toil, strife, and ultimately death in Genesis 3. Yet God is not distant from us in our affliction and the grind of life. He is still present and very much active.

God is standing behind us, even in the hardship of this life. His ultimate plan for your life is that He will be glorified in all things, and He will give you strength according to that end. Just look at the promise of Philippians 4:19–20: "And my God will supply every need of yours according to his riches in glory in Christ Jesus. To our God and Father be glory forever and ever. Amen."

God is your source of strength and grace when all the trappings of this world fail you. He is your supply; all you need to do is ask and He will grant you what you need according to His will. He is for you and with you. He has what you need for the next minute, the next hour, or the next day. All you need to do is ask.

Our prayer life does not have to be the sum of broken thoughts and the few prayers that we offer over our meals. We can pray unceasingly while still being an active participant in our jobs and families by finding the openings that each day has so that we can be people of prayer. There is no better way to endure in faith than to be in consistent conversation with the One we have trusted our lives to.

ABRAHAM

FAITH WHEN YOU CAN'T SEE

So Abram went, as the Lord had told him, and Lot went with him. Abram was seventy-five years old when he departed from Haran.

GENESIS 12:4

"So Abram went."

That simple phrase has been a balm to the heart of my family for years. God placed that verse on the heart of my wife Heather over a decade ago. We were praying through a ministry opportunity that would take us to western Arizona and had no idea what to do. This new opportunity seemed like a door that the Lord had clearly opened, but it also had some drawbacks that we were concerned about.

Both my wife and I had spent our entire lives in North Carolina. There is a significant culture difference between a Bible Belt state like North Carolina and the West Coast feel that Arizona has. Moving over two thousand miles away meant we would not be able to make it back home very much. Both sets of our parents were aging, and my dad had been diagnosed with stage three lung cancer the year before. Moving meant leaving the people we loved behind for an extended period of time.

The decision weighed heavily on us, and we had great difficulty trying to figure out what to do. In God's kindness, it just so happened that my wife was in a Bible study that was going through the entire book of Genesis. That study brought her to the call of Abram (later Abraham) in Genesis 12.

God's call on the life of Abraham was clear and full of promise, but his call would also lead him away from everything he had ever known into a land that he had never seen. Following the call of God meant he was going to have to leave his extended family behind that he loved. We don't know how Abraham weighed his options or how many sleepless nights it took for him to decide to uproot his life to go to the place that God had for him. All we know is that God called and Abraham went. A clear call was met with bold, faithful obedience.

So we went. That passage was an encouragement and a reminder of the faithfulness of God during that decision point and even today. We look at Abraham often as we worry about the path set out for us. In the times where we wonder why God is slow to act in our own eyes, we look at the patience that Abraham showed as he waited for a promised heir. Abraham's story is of a life that is chock-full of promises and faith as he waits for those promises to unfold.

In this chapter, we will look at the witness of Abraham. He had moments of both faith and failure, but he waited on the promises of God with a notable faith. He knew the promises that God had for him, but he had no idea of the endurance he would need in order to get to that place. Abraham is an example of navigating the long road in a faithful life.

Let's look at seven truths from Abraham's faith that can help us along our own journey.

ABRAHAM BELIEVED GOD'S WORD

Now the LORD said to Abram, "Go from your country and your
kindred and your father's house to the land that I will show
you. And I will make of you a great nation, and I will bless you
and make your name great, so that you will be a blessing. I will
bless those who bless you, and him who dishonors you I will
curse, and in you all the families of the earth shall be blessed."
GENESIS 12:1-3

The only assurance Abram had for his call to obedience were
the words God gave him. There was no burning bush. There
was no pillar of cloud by day and pillar of fire by night to follow.
There was no intense interaction with the Lord like Paul had
on the road to Damascus. God laid out what He wanted Abram
to do and He laid out the promises that He would uphold by
His own power. That was it.

Apparently, all Abram needed was the promise and direction of God to start packing up his entire life. Abram believed
that God was going to do as He said and that was the foundation of every action he took. Even in the verses following,
verses 7 and 8, he built an altar to the Lord whenever the Lord
spoke to him. He wanted to remember and honor the words
that the Lord had said and was already fulfilling.

This is a critical lesson for all of us. Abram took God at
His word. He believed what God promised and lived out the
call God gave him. At some previous point in Abram's life, the
Lord had shown Himself faithful to do what He said He would.
Clinging to the words of God is an important part of living out
a lifetime of faith.

The Scriptures, and the great cloud of witnesses contained
in them, reveal a God who is faithful to His promises and

covenants. He has never failed to do what He said He was going to do. The speed at which He fulfills His promises may seem slow in our eyes, but God always comes through. The faithful gospel thread that spans the Bible from Genesis to Revelation reminds us of God's plan and purpose. It is a plan that is always true and a purpose that has never been and will never be thwarted.

Abram modeled something else important for Christians: making monuments to God in moments of faithfulness. Abram went out of his way to build altars to honor God and His faithful work. We can do that today as believers. We do not have to stack up a bunch of stones to mark the faithfulness of God, but we can find reminders that mark the goodness, kindness, and faithfulness of God in our lives.

Marking the faithful word and work of God in our lives can be something we do daily as we take note of the grace of God. We can follow through on this by journaling the times that God's faithfulness has altered our lives in meaningful ways. This is a way for us to remember the faithfulness of God in our own lives so we can return to it in the times we feel most vulnerable. Take every effort to remember the faithfulness of God and His Word, as it can be the boost we need for the journey ahead.

ABRAHAM'S BELIEF WAS COUPLED WITH ACTION

So Abram went.

GENESIS 12:4

God's words in the first three verses of Genesis 12 gave Abram a lot to process. He was being asked to leave everything he knew for a place he had never seen for the sake of a multitude of descendants he would be blessed with, even though he was childless. Everything he was being asked to do was an ultimate exercise in faith toward God.

In spite of all the logical reasons not to do it, Abram got up and went anyway. His faith was grounded in belief. He believed that God was who He said He was, and he believed that God was going to do what He said. That belief was not the end of the story for Abram. The belief was the beginning. The obedience is what put flesh on his belief.

What we believe about God is vitally important. We should absorb every bit of truth and understanding that we can when it comes to the God we have entrusted our lives to, but faith cannot be just an academic exercise clothed in religiosity. What we have come to believe about God is our foundation, and what we do in view of that belief is our act of worship to the God we trust. Our trust in God cannot be just internal absorption. The work of God in the lives of those who trust Him has external evidence.

The challenge we face is not to stop at simply knowing God is good, kind, and faithful—but living like God is good, kind, and faithful. We must know whom our faith is placed in, and God pushes us to be people who live our lives in real ways. The faithfulness of God meant enough to Abram that he was not only comforted by it; he was driven by it. The God that he trusted his faith in was also the God he trusted his life and actions with.

A faith devoid of any discernable action is a faith that does not trust what it believes: "But be doers of the word, and not hearers only, deceiving yourselves" (James 1:22). Let us be people who follow through on what we hold dear. Let us be people who follow through on our word just as God has followed through on His. May we love grumpy people even as

Christ loved a sinful world enough to sacrifice Himself for it. Take that next hard step knowing that the God of all strength will be with you to help you.

Trust and do. Believe and live. This is what a life of faith is meant to look like: one that is believed and lived. We find ourselves on the journey of faith when what we believe about God presses us to live a life aimed at the purposes of God.

ABRAHAM KNEW THE DESTINATION, NOT THE DIRECTIONS

After these things God tested Abraham and said to him, "Abraham!" And he said, "Here I am." He said, "Take your son, your only son Isaac, whom you love, and go to the land of Moriah, and offer him there as a burnt offering on one of the mountains of which I shall tell you."

GENESIS 22:1-2

God unfolded a lot of promises to Abraham in Genesis 12. They were promises of descendants and a promise of a new place to call home. God was abundantly clear on what the destination was for Abraham. However, there was not as much detail when it came to how he was going to arrive at that place or how long it was going to take. The only thing that he knew was that God was going to get him there.

Fast forward to Genesis 22 where God tells Abraham to take his one and only son to the mountains. This father-son hike was not a stereotypical bonding moment because God was asking Abraham to sacrifice his son as an offering once they reached their destination. Abraham listened to what he was told. Abraham and his son Isaac hiked up the mountain. Abraham made the altar of wood and laid Isaac down on the altar. As he lifted the blade to stab his son, a voice of an angel stopped Abraham from killing his only heir.

At some point along that hike up the mountain, Abraham had to wonder what God was up to. Why would God want him to sacrifice his only son? How could God's promise come true if his only child was dead? There is plenty in this scenario that did not make earthly sense in the moment, but Abraham followed through and placed his hope in God.

Our lives are not much different than Abraham's when it comes to the promises of God. We know that He is with us and for us. We know that He loves us dearly. We know that Jesus has gone and prepared a place for us in glory. We know that the ultimate promise for His church is to be in His presence for eternity. However, the unknown lies in the details of everything that will unfold before that promise becomes reality.

Abraham did not know that his act of faith was a test of where his faith was placed. He certainly did not know that his act would become a living parable of the sacrifice the Father would make as He sent His Son to be crucified. Abraham did not know the why of the moment, but he knew the destination that God promised.

We often do not know the why of our difficulties. We do not understand why we have to face a myriad of health issues, financial stressors, and prisons of doubt in this life. There are times when we can see God's plan in our difficulties. In other situations, we won't understand the why until we see Jesus face to face.

Living out our faith means having to make decisions when we cannot see what is next. All we have is a snapshot of our final destination, and that is precisely the picture we need. We take that next step and make that next choice in view of our eternal purpose and destination. We rely on the faithfulness of God and try to live that out as best as we can. In the times where the directions do not make sense, we fix our eyes on the destination so we can take that next faithful step.

ABRAHAM'S PROMISE CAME WITH A COST

> *By faith Abraham obeyed when he was called to go out to a place that he was to receive as an inheritance. And he went out, not knowing where he was going. By faith he went to live in the land of promise, as in a foreign land, living in tents with Isaac and Jacob, heirs with him of the same promise.*
> **HEBREWS 11:8-9**

Abraham's call came with a wildly lavish inheritance, but it also came with an inherent cost. He said goodbye forever to people that he loved. He left behind his familiar and comfortable world for a land that was full to the brim of unknowns. He left a life of stability for one of transience. The cost of following the call of God was high, but the inheritance that lay beyond what Abraham could see was vast. He was willing to embrace the cost to grab on to something far more valuable.

This is the essence of discipleship: embracing the death of what I once had to grab hold of a new inheritance—the life and hope that I have because of Jesus. The cost of following Jesus means taking up a cross. The cross has become so much of a religious symbol that we forget it is an instrument of torture and death that we carry. Our call to follow our Lord comes with sacrifice—even everything if need be. As Jesus says, "So therefore, any one of you who does not renounce all that he has cannot be my disciple" (Luke 14:33).

Following the call of Christ involves taking an inventory of costs. Am I willing to give up my reputation, my wants, my loves, my money, my people, my comfort, or my resources to follow this Jesus? If I am not willing, I cannot be a disciple of Jesus. Either we make Jesus Lord of all or He is not Lord at all. Following the call of discipleship means adding up the costs and saying it is all still worth it.

Tally up the costs. Look at the inheritance to come. What you once had will pale in comparison to what is to come.

THE JOURNEY IS WORTH THE COST

Abraham breathed his last and died in a good old age, an old man and full of years, and was gathered to his people.
GENESIS 25:8

Abraham counted the costs and experienced loss on all sorts of levels. For all the uncertainty, all the wandering through the desert, all the goodbyes, all the doubt and every sacrifice made, I feel confident Abraham thought it was all worth it. God allowed him to have 175 years on this planet. He arrived at his 175th year able to say that his life was well lived. He now had a glimpse of the people who would bless the world because of his faithful journey. He could go to his Master in peace knowing that it was all worth it.

Many of those found in the list of faithful people in Hebrews 11 would say the same thing, as well as others who grace the pages of Scripture. Countless figures in the timeline of the Bible faced extensive losses: jobs, respect, homes, possessions, worldly comforts, meaningful relationships, and even their very lives. Yet, those same people who lost so much knew their inheritance was worth it.

Paul was one of those people who lost a wealth of things. In spite of that, Paul says, "Indeed, I count everything as loss because of the surpassing worth of knowing Christ Jesus my Lord. For his sake I have suffered the loss of all things and count them as rubbish, in order that I may gain Christ" (Philippians 3:8). Paul looks across the landscape of his life and all of the things that were once his. As he gathers them up in his mind, their sum is but mere trash in view of what Jesus has gained him.

The days that we walk in might not be filled with any sort of tangible richness, yet that is not where the believer can find lasting hope. We look to the promise of eternity with our Lord. We look to the surpassing worth that we have already in being redeemed and adopted. We look to the promises fulfilled and the promises yet to come knowing that it has been, and will be, worth it.

THE WAIT IS HARD AND LONG

For when God made a promise to Abraham, since he had no one greater by whom to swear, he swore by himself, saying, "Surely I will bless you and multiply you." And thus Abraham, having patiently waited, obtained the promise.
HEBREWS 6:13-15

Abraham did more than simply wait. His wait was one of epic proportions. From the time that Abraham was promised to have descendants to the time he became the father of Isaac, twenty-five years passed. He had to wait an agonizing two and a half decades of an already long life before God's promise became real. He did not just wait on the Lord; he "patiently waited." The Greek word here means to persevere patiently and bravely in enduring misfortunes and troubles.

Abraham waited until it hurt. He waited knowing that more hurt was on the way. He embodied the house built on the firm foundation (Matthew 7:24–27). The storms of life swept into his world. The rains came and the wind howled, but the house stood. Abraham heard what the Lord was set to do, and Abraham followed through on what the Lord God asked of him. Only by faith was he able to patiently wait.

It is hard to wait on the Lord when we can look around and see wicked people snapping up worldly fortune day after day. We pray, cry, and call out but see no forward momentum in our faith or in our lives. Waiting when it seems like we are going nowhere is a brutal burden to bear. We have no desire to face any sort of misfortune because we don't have any worldly fortune left to give. Waiting for a movement of the Lord is hard in any situation, much less in tribulation.

While Abraham is a standout example of longsuffering and patience, the weight of the verses from Hebrews 6 are placed on God Himself. It is God's oath and God's promises that carried Abraham along as he waited and endured. In the worst of the wait, God's sovereign hand upholds our weary heads as we wait for the promise of seeing our Lord face to face.

GOD IS FAITHFUL EVEN WHEN WE ARE NOT

And Sarai said to Abram, "Behold now, the Lord *has prevented me from bearing children. Go in to my servant; it may be that I shall obtain children by her." And Abram listened to the voice of Sarai.*

GENESIS 16:2

Though Abraham was characterized as a man of faith, he did have moments where his fear led him to take things into his own hands. While waiting on their promised child, Sarai and Abram became concerned that the promise would not be fulfilled. In their impatience, Abram slept with his wife's servant Hagar, which almost instantly spawned strife in their family and did not fulfill God's promise.

Abram assumed in the moment that his covenant with God was his to uphold, which was not true. Just as God upholds His people in their waiting, so God will also uphold His promises and covenants. God does not need the underhanded efforts of people to accomplish His ultimate mission—He has the means for His mission.

Yet, Abraham assumed the role and mantle of God in Genesis 16. Abraham lied about the identity of his wife to Pharaoh in Genesis 12. In the span of a few chapters, Abraham was making a habit of disobeying the ordinances of God to try to meet his own ends. In doing so, Abraham suffers the consequences of his fear and choices by having his life become more complicated. Yet, as Abraham failed, the works and promises of God prevailed.

God is a Father who deals with the sins of His children with discipline, as any loving father would (Hebrews 12:6), but He is also forgiving, "merciful and gracious, slow to anger and abounding in steadfast love" (Psalm 103:8). He is patient toward us so that we may ultimately come to a place of repentance.

God knows every bit of the sin that we walked in before we trusted in Jesus as our Savior, and He also knows every iniquity that we will walk in for the days to come. In view of all of that, the Father still chooses to adopt you. He still chooses to forgive you and use you as a vessel of grace in all the world. Even the good works we live out are ones that He has prepared beforehand for us to walk in (Ephesians 2:10). God sees all your sins and even sets you up to walk in the things that honor Him—and He still loves you.

There are so many times when we think that we have lived a life that disqualifies us from the service of God: we have sinned too many times, we have made too many mistakes, and we have too few spiritual gifts for God to love us or to want to use us. Yet, God does not distance Himself from you because of the life you have lived. He draws near to those who are humble and in full awareness of their need for Him. He is faithful to us even when we have failed His decrees. Don't pull away from God in the wake of your failures; draw near to Him in humility and watch Him redeem the most broken of circumstances for His glory.

CHAPTER 6

MADE FOR COMMUNITY

Two are better than one, because they have a good reward
for their toil. For if they fall, one will lift up his fellow.
But woe to him who is alone when he falls and has not
another to lift him up!
ECCLESIASTES 4:9-10

My entrance into college was a point of growth for me on a lot of levels. It was the first time I was out from under the watchful care of my parents for an extended period of time. I was making adult decisions without the guardrails of parental insight. I had to do daily "grown-up" tasks that make a life run: cook, clean, pay bills, and do laundry. To say I faced a steep learning curve when it came to cooking might be the understatement of the millennium. I had a lot of experiential training in adulthood in those first few months of my freshman year.

I had to grow up academically as well. I double majored at The College at Southeastern in biblical studies and the history of ideas. The latter is basically a Christian worldview studies program. We read and studied a large section of books that helped shape Western thought and then examined what we read in light of the faith we held. Reading was not something I was well-versed in. As a participant of North Carolina public schools, reading through weighty thought was low on the priority list of our education.

On top of all that, I needed to grow on just about every level socially. I am naturally introverted, and I will rarely put myself out there for people whom I have not built trust with. That was a problem since I had moved to a new city and attended a school where I did not know anyone. I struggled mightily in that first year to open up and make friends, but I had no one to blame but myself.

After I finished my freshman year at Southeastern, I did what every good Christian college student does: I worked at a Christian camp over the summer. The camp I worked at was called Snowbird Wilderness Outfitters, and it suited me perfectly. This camp loved Jesus, they loved teaching teenagers the Bible, and they loved the outdoors. Working there was a dream scenario for me, and I was certain I was going to enjoy the summer.

One aspect of being there that I did not anticipate was the community I built with other believers. A lot of that simply had to do with the structure of the camp. All the staff were in college, all the staff were believers, and a vast majority of the staff at the time were praying through a future either in ministry or missions. Putting a hundred college students together with that level of commonality creates an instant bond.

There was more than just commonality though. We had a family bond that was cemented through living together for three months. We shared bunkrooms. We ate nearly every meal together. We spent our time off together exploring the mountains of North Carolina. Our proximity deepened our bonds and love for one another.

It was also at Snowbird that I saw the imagery of the body of Christ play out. Jesus was the cornerstone of everything that went on there. He was the reason why we sweated through summer days to have fun with students we had just met. He was the reason why we stayed up late into the night talking with kids who were hurting. Jesus was the reason we were spending our summer in the mountains with a bunch of middle school students instead of being back in our hometowns with our friends.

We celebrated birthdays and engagements together as a big group. We grieved tribulations and loss as a group. We pitched in if we saw another staff member struggling in their daily job. We built up our friends when they were going through a bad day. We were one big awkward group, but we were a family brought together because of what Jesus had done.

My four summers there made a lasting impact on my life. Some of my best friends and closest brothers in ministry came from my time there. I ended up meeting my wife Heather at Snowbird. Seeing her work there made me fall in love with her. I fell in love with her as I watched her love others, even when she was worn out. I watched her carefully and lovingly listen to teenage girls as they talked to her about the struggles they were facing. I had the chance to see my future wife for everything that she was. There was no pretense to who she was. There was no time or energy for that. I fell in love with Heather because I got to know so much of who she was as an adopted daughter in the family of God.

The biblical community from four summers at that camp changed my life not only in relationships gained but also in regard to how I pursued relationships to come. I saw the power that came from listening to others when they were hurting. I saw the power that the ministry of presence has in the lives of others. My next two decades of ministry were molded by the fact that the church must be built on Christians seeing the love of Christ toward them and then finding practical ways to extend that same love to others they encounter.

This need for community is not new. It is not something brought on by the social media age that we live in today. We can see the need from the very beginning in the words of the Father: "It is not good that the man should be alone" (Genesis 2:18). God made Adam with a need for community, which is why God gave him Eve as both his companion and helper.

The world has changed a lot from the days of Adam and Eve, but our need for companionship and help has not. God knows our hearts, and He has not left us alone. He is with us and for us, but He has also given us a visible manifestation of His love through His church. We cannot afford to miss our opportunity to see the beauty in and power of the community that God has given us through His church. Let us look at some rhythms that we can put into action in our lives right now that will help us live in community as God intended.

BE PART OF A LOCAL CHURCH

When the COVID-19 lockdowns began, seemingly overnight, we went from being able to go to worship services at a local church to having to watch a streamed service in our homes. In those first few weeks of self-isolation, it was a true blessing to still hear my pastor preach and to be able to worship in the middle of my living room while singing along with my church's worship team. As much of a blessing as those days were, it was not the same. There was something missing.

There is no substitute for the gathering of God's people. While I could see my pastor and my worship team, they could not see me. Every Sunday when I logged in to our livestream, I could see the count of the other households that were logged into the watch. I could see a number, but I could not see a face. I could not smile and catch up with my friends that I worshiped with. I could not pray over a buddy that I knew was having a tough week. I could not give an assuring hug to those I counted as dear friends.

I had the chance to see a church worship service, but I was still missing out on the opportunity to gather as God's people. There is not a viable substitute for the physical gathering of God's church. There are so many aspects of gathering that cannot be done in a virtual environment. God intended for His church to be together in a physical location, investing in each other's lives, not gathering for a virtual experience. We were meant to weep with the hurting and pray for those who are burdened. That cannot happen without face to face interaction, and it will never happen as we passively watch a screen. That is why the author of Hebrews was explicit in saying we should not make a habit of being distant from one another: "And let us consider how to stir up one another to love and good works, not neglecting to meet together, as is the habit of some, but encouraging one another, and all the more as you see the Day drawing near" (Hebrews 10:24–25).

Our opportunity to consider the needs of one another is heightened when we can see one another on a regular basis. It affords us the chance to see what is going on in the lives of others that a simple text message could never show. We can see the joy in someone's eyes or the weight that is sitting on someone's shoulders. We can engage our church family in ways that a phone call or a Zoom meeting never can.

That is why we are called to gather. Find a church in your community and city. Go and gather there every week. Worship and sit under biblically based preaching. Find a way to engage other people and to encourage them. The gathering of the church is a meeting of people who follow the same Lord and share the same hope. That is a tangible reminder that we need regularly. We are not alone. Many other people love whom we love and seek to serve whom we serve. The gathering of the church has a power of presence that virtual meetings never will.

MAKE CHURCH MEMBERSHIP MEANINGFUL

While the gathering of God's church is vital, there is also a deeper level to being a part of God's church than mere attendance. We must be committed to God's church through membership. Church membership is a formal relationship between a church and a person. In entering this relationship, the church affirms the person's confession of faith and takes responsibility for that person's discipleship. Likewise, the prospective member seeks to serve the church and submits to its leadership.

Church membership in many ways is covenantal in nature. The church bears the weight of the covenant while the member vows to pursue faithfulness to the church. It takes the consistent attendance to the gathering of believers to another level as now consistency is met with commitment. It ties the believer to a people and not just to a time or place. Church membership takes a person as a part and joins them to the whole.

> The eye cannot say to the hand, "I have no need of you," nor again the head to the feet, "I have no need of you." On the contrary, the parts of the body that seem to be weaker are indispensable, and on those parts of the body that we think less honorable we bestow the greater honor, and our unpresentable parts are treated with greater modesty, which our more presentable parts do not require. But God has so composed the body, giving

greater honor to the part that lacked it, that there may be no division in the body, but that the members may have the same care for one another. If one member suffers, all suffer together; if one member is honored, all rejoice together." (1 Corinthians 12:21–26)

In joining a church as a member, the individual is committing to a people, not a pastor. So even as leadership changes throughout the seasons of life, the allegiance of the members does not. They are united to the body of Christ by the work of Christ and not the words of the pastor. In this covenant relationship the church pledges to care for the Christian and the Christian pledges to care for the church.

Much like the commitment in a marriage ceremony, the Christian is committed to their local church through the good times and bad, through the seasons of growth and waning momentum. For better or worse, the member remains even when other local churches have better preaching, a bigger youth group, or a more vibrant women's ministry. The Christian not only chooses to gather but to remain faithful to a local church so that they may be a part of a larger and more vibrant body.

BE WILLING TO GO SMALL

The majority (59 percent) of churches in the United States have less than 100 attendees on a given Sunday, while 35 percent of churches have less than 500 weekly worshipers. Those congregations do not seem overly large, but when seen through the lens of personal interaction, the numbers seem daunting.

To put it another way: How many people in your church do you know by name? Do you know all the names of their family members? Their ages? When we get down to that level of intimacy, there are limits to how much we can really know a person just by joining them in worship. Odds are that we do not know the majority of people very well that we worship with on Sunday, and likewise they do not know us.

If we are not careful, we can attend church without ever having the church get to know us. The church of God was never meant to be a transactional appointment on our calendar. It is a body of people that we relate to. But the Sunday worship gathering is a poor facilitator of relationship. Often the play-by-play of our Sunday gatherings can be summarized as: walk into church, exchange pleasantries, sing corporately, pray corporately, sit under the preaching of God's Word, and then go home. That Sunday rhythm scarcely affords us the opportunity to be known by others or to get to know the people who call our same church "home."

For this reason, many churches offer smaller gatherings of believers. Depending on your church context, these gatherings might be called community groups, small groups, or Sunday School (for you Bible Belt folks). These groups exist for the purpose of studying Scripture, praying for one another, and getting to know other believers on a more intimate level. They offer the chance for questions and discussion. They are an outlet where the Christian is an active participant and not just passively present.

Jesus Himself shepherded people in the same way. He would go out and teach the message of God to the masses. When He finished this corporate teaching, He would often pull His twelve disciples to the side so that He could teach them and talk with them further. On an even deeper level, Jesus would take three of those disciples (Peter, James, and John) with Him to teach them even more (Matthew 26:37).

There is great value in being known and knowing others. While it is crucial for us to gather in the large assembly of believers in worship, it is also important for us to come together in smaller groups to be able to exhort one another in our faith. It takes time to establish relational and spiritual momentum in a group of people, but it is an investment of energy and time that pays off in the long run.

BE VULNERABLE AND HONEST

Being with the gathered church as well as spending time together with small groups has a tremendous amount of value for the building up of the Christian. The large service allows us to better know the God we love while small groups allow us to get to know the church that we are seeking to love. However, the encouragement that comes from being in the community of a small group will be limited if we hide what is going on in our lives and the lives of our family members.

Consider your introductory conversations with fellow church members when you walk into a weekly worship service or small group. Most people we know will come over to say hello and then inevitably ask us, "How are you?" Many of us will have a generalized answer prepared in the back of our minds along the lines of: "I'm good. How are you?" That may be a true statement, or that statement may be hiding the hurt that the past week has levied on your weary soul.

It feels like there is an unspoken pressure in the American church to be perfect. We feel the pressure to press forward as if everything in our lives is okay. We will go through all our conversations with other believers acting like there is no trouble with our marriage, our children, our jobs, or our faith, even when there is an issue. The pressure to appear perfect is present in the church because Satan wants the people of God to feel isolated in their brokenness.

We do not have to buy the lie that we cannot be open about what is going on in our lives—whether that is sharing the graces God is showering you with or being vulnerable about the affliction that you are trying to live through. God gave us the church so that His mission will be accomplished but also so that the people of God will have the support they need to live in this broken world.

God intends for you to share your life and even your burdens with the people you call your brothers and sisters in Christ. God charges His church to do this in Galatians 6:2: "Bear one another's burdens, and so fulfill the law of Christ." Strength can come from sharing the weakness you find yourself in. Seek out people you can trust and whom you love. When you find those people, make sure they know what is going on in your life so that they can love you, stand behind you, and pray for you.

FIND WAYS TO SERVE

As each has received a gift, use it to serve one another, as good stewards of God's varied grace: whoever speaks, as one who speaks oracles of God; whoever serves, as one who serves by the strength that God supplies—in order that in everything God may be glorified through Jesus Christ. To him belong glory and dominion forever and ever. Amen.

1 PETER 4:10-11

Like we saw earlier, God arranged His church in such a way that each member needs all the others. We are each a part of the church, and we all have a unique gifting by which we can serve the church. The church is the place where we can use our gifts to glorify God and care for His people.

Finding a way to serve the local church can be difficult. I have the spiritual gift of teaching, but I also have struggled to serve my local church given the rhythms of my ministry. Every weekend, I am traveling and speaking at churches all over the country, so I am rarely at my home church. With that sort of schedule, I cannot have a consistent role leading any sort of small group at my church, but God has given me other opportunities.

A couple of years ago, my church was in need of people to lead and teach Bible lessons at our Vacation Bible School (VBS). When I heard about the opportunity, I was hesitant because I am not good with little kids. I struggle to teach Scripture on a fourth-grade level, and kids struggle to understand where my arms went. It is a match made in heaven.

It just so happened that my schedule was wide open the week our Vacation Bible School was set to happen. I had no excuse not to do it apart from my feelings of inadequacy. With every logical reason not to do it removed, I reluctantly signed up to teach a class of nine-year-old boys. Looking back, I do not regret the decision one bit. I got to know some amazing kids, I grew in my ability to teach kids that age, and God was ultimately glorified through the week.

Our excuses for not serving the church of God are confined to our view of the power of God. If He can call us from spiritual death to spiritual life, then He can use our lives to show the world His goodness. All we have to do is to be willing—willing to teach, willing to change diapers in the nursery, willing to greet, willing to be on the sound team, or willing to sweat through VBS. The church of God needs all its parts, using all of its abilities within the body of Christ. The sacrifice of service makes God look glorious.

SUPPORT AND SUBMIT TO
CHURCH LEADERSHIP

Leadership is often very lonely. Church leadership often has that feeling of loneliness multiplied a few times over. Many church members do not see the laundry list of tasks a pastor has to accomplish in a given week. They see him preach the Sunday sermon, but they do not see the hours of preparation and prayer that went into that sermon. They see him greet a family in the church lobby, but they do not see the hours of crisis marriage counseling that he did with that same family this week. They see him ask for people to give toward the weekly offering, but they do not see him fretting over the monthly budget to keep the church running.

First and foremost, your pastor needs the support of your prayer. The weight of the office of elder and pastor leads many into unrelenting emotional and spiritual stress. It is an office that can keep leaders away from their families at dinner and bedtime. Many early mornings are spent with church members having breakfast and talking life at a local coffee shop. Their cell phones rarely have a time without a call to return or an email or text to reply to. In serving people, their jobs are never done, and rarely is there a visible manifestation of a job well done. Their to-do list is never done, so pray for your pastors because they need it.

Secondly, submit to the pastor and elders of your church. Often the decisions they have to make will cause someone in the church to be upset with them, which is not their end goal. They know that God will call them into account for every decision they make and for every word they teach. They make decisions with the ultimate goal of God being glorified and the gospel being spread by how you function as a church. As the author of Hebrews says in Hebrews 13:17, "Obey your leaders and submit to them, for they are keeping watch over your souls, as those who will have to give an account. Let them do this with joy and not with groaning, for that would be of no advantage to you."

It does us and them no good for the congregants to be social media snipers about every decision they make. God has given them the authority at this place and time for a purpose (Romans 13:1). As long as our pastors and elders continue to stay true to the gospel that is laid out in Scripture, let us be a church that prays for and follows them.

Yet, there is an important caveat here when we say as long as elders "stay true to the gospel," because that is not a guarantee. Some pastors depart from biblical teaching and proclaim ideas that Scripture never says. Some church leaders abuse their authority or abuse others. In cases like this, you have no reason to submit to wayward or abusive leadership. Expose sins like this, call for accountability, and do not allow poor leadership to carry on.

LOVE YOUR CHURCH LIKE YOUR FAMILY

There is a familial aspect of the New Testament church that often gets overlooked by the modern church. We can fall into the trap of seeing the church as a physical place where the people of God gather to worship. The Scriptures remind us that the church is a people God has gathered through the sacrifice of His Son. By His sacrifice all of the church is adopted into the family of God (Romans 8:15).

This act of adoption not only gives us a Heavenly Father, but we are also brought into an adopted family of brothers and sisters who are united by the saving work of Jesus—the church. This relationship is not only transactional but familial. Peter reminds the church of this in 1 Peter 1:22: "Having purified your souls by your obedience to the truth for a sincere brotherly love, love one another earnestly from a pure heart." The charge is to love one another like the spiritual family that we already are.

The ways we can love the church like our family are almost limitless. We can meet the physical and monetary needs of our church family when we see them arise. We can speak words of encouragement as we see opportunity. We can invite people and families over to our house to share a meal and a laugh. Think of the ways you love the family you have by blood and find ways to bring that to life in the family you have by the blood of Christ.

This sort of love makes the church of God stand out from the rest of the world. To love others as much as they love themselves is a call that is distinct from how the rest of the world operates. Jesus speaks of this distinct love from disciple to disciple in John 13:35: "By this all people will know that you are my disciples, if you have love for one another." The familial love from disciple to disciple is a missional act by the church of God.

Being community is not easy. Gathering a bunch of broken people who are prone to sin is a recipe for hurt and heartache. However, God has brought His church together through more than just our preferences or proximity. God has brought His church together through the work of Jesus on the cross and His adoption of believers into the family of God. Like any family, the church of God takes work, but the work is worth it. We gather, love, serve, and share knowing that we will grow and God will be glorified—now and as we endure in our faith in the future.

CHAPTER 7

MADE FOR KINSHIP

Your wife will be like a fruitful vine within your house; your children will be like olive shoots around your table.

PSALM 128:3

In the fall of 2018 I made the switch from being a student pastor to a full-time speaker and evangelist. In terms of the skill set required and the aim, not much changed about what I was doing. Both in my former and new role I communicated to others what the hope of the gospel means for their lives. While the core of what I did remained the same, the means and location of my job changed dramatically.

As a student pastor, I served my local church week in and week out. Aside from student trips like summer camp, mission trips, or fall retreat, everything we did was either at our church or my wife and I would host small group studies in our home. The rhythm of my ministry life in those days meant that my family was a part of my work, or I was at least home at night to see my wife and kids before they went to bed.

That all changed once I began my career as a speaker. My speaking and preaching engagements quickly went from being based in North Carolina to spreading to churches across the southeastern United States. My speaking in 2019 carried me to 15 states, preaching or speaking 112 times, traveling over 42,000 miles, and being on the road for a total of 170 days. I love what God has called me to do, and I am incredibly grateful for the ministry opportunities He has given me. It has been very clear that the grace of God is working in and through the ministry. He is doing things and opening doors I could not possibly do with my own strength and smarts.

Though God's hand was working in the ministry, it was also clear I had some real challenges to deal with when it came to that level of travel, but it had nothing to do with the ministry structure; it had everything to do with how I was investing in my family. Not only was I juggling a busy ministry calendar, but I also had a wife at home along with two kids who were seven and four years old at the time. It did not take long for us to realize that even at that young age, the kids felt a void when I was gone for days on end. It was felt by my wife who had to care for the kids, the dog, the house, and the errands for half of the year while I was gone. I saw that being a meaningful part of my kids' lives and being a help to my wife was going to take deliberate effort on my part.

Every weekend, I typically travel hundreds of miles, speak multiple times, and meet scores of people face to face. It is hard to be "on" for all of that and then head home while being "on" for my wife and kids. If my family are the most important people in my life, do they not deserve more from me than what I give to people I have never met? The answer is yes, they do. My family deserves just as much attention, effort, and empathy as the people who employ me. In fact, for those of us in ministry, there is a greater burden placed on who we are under our own roof than who we are at the pulpit. The requirements for the office of church elder in Titus 1 have more to do with being a faithful Christian, husband, and father than they do with being an expositor of the Bible. How I serve the people under my roof matters, and serving them well means having a grasp of what is going on in their hearts and lives.

Halfway through my busy ministry season in 2019, I noticed something was off with my son Teague. After sitting and talking with him, I figured out he was missing his daddy. He is my mini-me. He follows me around the house, loves to watch the sports I watch, and wants to tell me about his day every day. My busyness had left a hole in the heart of my little boy, and I needed to figure out how I could give him the quality time his heart needed.

There was not a whole lot of room in my speaking schedule for time with just him and me, but there was a way that I could bring him into what I was doing. I was scheduled to speak in July of that year at Chestnut Mountain Ranch, a boys' home tucked away in the mountains of West Virginia. Teague had just gotten to the age where I knew he would sit still while I spoke and not hinder what I was being brought in to do. I also knew that this was a chance to invest in my son while providing him an opportunity to learn about how this boys' home showed the love of Jesus to kids in their greatest time of need.

It was exactly the trip we both needed. We had fun exploring all the Appalachian Mountains had to offer. We stopped at the North Carolina-Virginia border and took goofy selfies at the "Virginia Is for Lovers" sign. We saw the New River Gorge Bridge, one of the largest single-span arch bridges in the United States. We hiked around the Gauley River and took pictures of river otters. We sang John Mayer's live album from his Nokia Theatre show—*Where the Light Is*—at the top of our lungs while we drove through the mountains. We had an absolute blast.

We had fun, but we talked a lot too. We talked about what a boys' home is and what it meant for the boys who lived at Chestnut Mountain Ranch. We talked about why "religion that is pure and undefiled before God the Father is this: to visit orphans and widows in their affliction" (James 1:27). We heard story after story of how both the staff and boys at the home had seen the clear manifestation of God's love during their time there.

These memories and lessons are seared into the memory of my son, but so are the less spectacular rhythms of our family's everyday life. We love the people that we know the best—spouses, kids, parents, college roommates, close friends—by taking deliberate steps to meet their needs and love them even when we have excuses not to. Let us take a look at some ways we can love the people who are with us for the long run, no matter what may come.

SPEAK LOVE

A few lessons stand out over the years of doing funerals in the churches that I have served in. One of the sad realities is many close family members and friends wish they would have told the departed what they really meant to them. Those words are often spoken for the first time over a casket in a eulogy instead of to the person face to face over a cup of coffee.

It may be a grim reminder, but we have a tendency to assume the people we love the most know exactly what we think about them. While many people know that we love them, they may not know what we love and appreciate about them. That is precisely the encouragement and affirmation people need from those that mean the most to them.

Especially for men it can be hard to express emotions and feelings, but expressing love toward others can feel foreign and uncomfortable for us all at times. Yet God charges us to be vocal in showing love in Romans 12:10: "Love one another with brotherly affection. Outdo one another in showing honor."

We are to have "brotherly affection." Yes, men and women should talk about how they feel about others. God even makes it a competition by charging us to "outdo" one another in how we show honor. That is the sort of competition I think we can all get behind.

Do not let time pass before you tell the people who matter to you most that you love them and why you love them. They may already know, but assuming they know can fracture hearts. Our heavenly Father speaks His love for His children over and over and over, and we should take a hint from His lead. Frail human hearts need a constant reminder of who loves them and how they are loved. Let us show that love through our words to the people who mean the most to us.

BE ENGAGED BY ASKING QUESTIONS

In my more than a decade of working with teenagers, one complaint came up constantly: "I don't feel like my parents get me." These kids were from different home environments, but in each situation distance had grown between the student and the parents. The perceived distance and isolation were fracturing the student's belief that their parents understood who they were, and it caused their trust in their parents to crater.

Our chance to engage with the people we love can be as simple as checking in on someone. This is not meant to be an act of prying. It is more of an opportunity to see what is going on in their life. It can be as simple as asking how someone's day went or as complex as talking to them about their most recent failure or success. Helping someone feel understood often comes from us being emotionally and physically present.

Paul challenges fathers to "not provoke your children to anger" (Ephesians 6:4), which is easier said than done. Kids can get set off for all sorts of reasons, especially in the teenage years. I think of the times when my little ones are the angriest at me, and it almost always comes back to them not understanding a choice I made or feeling like I do not understand something they are trying to express to me. Many of these frustrating times could have been avoided if I had just asked a couple of questions.

We can wipe away dangerous assumptions in any given relationship if we are consistent in checking on the people we love. Ask people how they are really doing or ask how things are going in your relationship. Remove hindrances of the heart by seeking clarity and staying engaged with the lives of those you love the most. Ask about what they love. Ask about what they hate. Ask about how they know that God loves them. Whatever way you go about it, just ask to be an engaged part of the lives you love.

START DISCIPLESHIP AT HOME

We just read the first part of Paul's challenge to fathers in Ephesians 6:4: "Do not provoke your children to anger." The second part of that challenge is just as succinct, but easily overlooked. Paul says of fathers and children to "bring them up in the discipline and instruction of the Lord."

That charge seems innocuous, but there are troubled waters that surround this plea thanks to the church culture today. If I am honest, I was part of the problem two decades ago. At the beginning of the millennium, student ministry within many churches was built on giving teens a "safe place" to be themselves. The thought was that teens would not come to church and be themselves if their parents were around. By keeping parents at a distance, the unspoken message was that parents should leave the discipleship of their kids to the professionals. The fallout of this ministry philosophy led to student discipleship becoming dependent on the few hours a week that a teen was at church while the world had the rest of the week to disciple them.

The results were disastrous. This youth ministry philosophy led to huge numbers of teens coming to church, but it also produced a small number of disciples. Thankfully, the pendulum has swung the other way in many youth ministries here in the United States recently. By seeing both the need for sustainable discipleship as well as the biblical burden for parents to be the primary disciple-makers of their kids, the culture has made a turn.

Many of the parents I talk to feel inadequate to be *the person* the discipleship of their student is dependent on, but like we will see in a couple of chapters, discipleship is dependent on investment of time and not perfection. In both Ephesians 6 and Deuteronomy 6:7 you are called to "teach [God's commands] diligently to your children." The call is to make the effort to impress the truth of God's character onto the hearts of your kids.

Read through a page or two of *The Jesus Storybook Bible* with your kids if they are little. Read a short section of Scripture with your kids and talk about it. Watch a YouTube sermon from a pastor you enjoy and talk through it as a family. The options are limitless when it comes to sharing the truth of God's Word with your children. You do not have to be perfect. All you need to do is to keep trying.

TALK ABOUT GOD WHEN THE OPPORTUNITY PRESENTS ITSELF

Both my kids are talkers, which was a little bit trying when COVID-19 swept across the country. We were all huddled up in the house together day after day, and both my kids wanted to do nothing but talk to me. They would follow me into the kitchen, to go get the mail, while I was on a call for work, and even while I brushed my teeth. When they had their fill of talking to my wife and me, they would scale the privacy fence in our backyard to try to talk to all of our neighbors.

With that level of conversational inundation, there are times when their conversation takes a decidedly spiritual turn. They are curious about prayer or they wonder why God made their dad without arms while they still have both their arms. Yet, these faith conversations extend beyond the bounds of their curiosity and questioning. We watch life play out on a daily basis as people make choices that honor God or that choose self over Savior. Those are the moments when we can talk about what following Jesus really looks like out in the world.

That is why the call for discipleship in Deuteronomy 6:8 carries past the one-time teaching of God's commands: "Talk of them when you sit in your house, and when you walk by the way, and when you lie down, and when you rise." Every day grants us the opportunity to talk about who God is and how He changes everything about our lives, but we must be watching for the conversational seams in our day to bring Him up.

It is vitally important that both our kids and the people closest to us see that God is worthy of being talked about every day of the week, not just Sunday. Otherwise we subconsciously reinforce the sacred and secular divide by keeping all things spiritual within the confines of Sunday while the rest of the week is spent with our faith going unmentioned.

Be willing to share the moments of God's grace you experience in a given day. Be willing to talk about what God is teaching you through your study of Scripture. Wrestle through how current events match up with a biblically based worldview. Seize every opportunity to let the words of your mouth and the meditations of your heart be acceptable in God's sight (Psalm 19:14). Talk about the most important person in your life so that anyone listening can get a taste of the goodness of God, just as you have.

REST WITH YOUR BEST PEOPLE

Thus the heavens and the earth were finished, and all the host of them. And on the seventh day God finished his work that he had done, and he rested on the seventh day from all his work that he had done. So God blessed the seventh day and made it holy, because on it God rested from all his work that he had done in creation.

GENESIS 2:1-3

Rest matters.

Rest is something that many of us lost hold of long ago. We have become people who are programmed to go until bedtime and then rise in the morning to do it all over again. This cycle carries on from day to day with no end in sight until sickness or a life event stops us—and for many of us the pause is welcomed. There is something life-giving about stillness.

We are both made and commanded to rest for a time each week, though many of us have gotten out of the habit of doing so. God knows our hearts desire going and doing, which is why from the very beginning He gave us a model to follow.

God gave both the example and the command (Exodus 20:8) for humanity to set aside a day for rest, which for some is a hard thing to do. Work schedules can be odd and resting on a Saturday or Sunday may be an impossibility. When I was a student pastor, the weekends were my busiest time. Saturday was for sermon prep, and I worked hard all day Sunday. There was little rest in my weekend rhythms, but that is why I structured my schedule to be off on Fridays.

With a little creativity, we can find a solution to rest. Our bodies and our souls need the pause to refresh and the time to be still. The people we love need dedicated time with us where our attention is not pulled away by another text message or email. Just as the Father set the example for His children, so we should set the example for ours. Our hope is not dependent on our works but on His finished work. We can take time to be still so that we may see the work of His hands and rest in His work that won our hope.

SAY I'M SORRY

Years ago, one of the students at my church pulled me to the side and asked if he could meet with me that week. He was on the verge of tears, so I knew it had to be serious. I feared the worst as I prayed over the conversation I was going to have with this teen. I tried my best to prepare for every possible scenario, but I had not prepared for the problem the student brought to me that afternoon.

This student walked into my office and very quietly sat down on my couch. After some small talk and a little bit of prying, he finally explained why he had come to my office that day. "How do you confess your sin? I just don't know how. I've never seen it done." He had me floored. The kid that sat in my office had a dad who was a deacon in our church and his mom was a Sunday School teacher, but he had never seen any public confession or repentance in his home.

Without ever having seen ownership and confession of sin, he was left without any sort of model to go on as to how to confess his sins. This left him with a significant hole in his understanding of the gospel. With no forgiveness being extended in his home, he figured there was no way God would forgive his sin. Matthew 6:14–15 loomed large in his conscience: "For if you forgive others their trespasses, your heavenly Father will also forgive you, but if you do not forgive others their trespasses, neither will your Father forgive your trespasses."

I sat with him for more than an hour talking about the biblical model of confession—how he could confess his sins to others as well as confessing and repenting of his sins before God. He felt a little better by the time we finished our conversation and he went on his way. Even so, the damage was done and had to be sorted through.

The reality of Ephesians 6 hangs over the leadership of every home. Our marriages and our parenting, especially as dads, are the living, breathing examples of the gospel for our kids and those around us. When it comes to saying "I'm sorry," the importance cannot be understated. Our families need to see confession and repentance in real life because we have a Savior who is faithful to forgive.

May we be people who seek restoration when we have offended one another. May we be leaders who can see when we are wrong and own it. May we be people of forgiveness, for the gospel's sake.

CELEBRATE WHAT YOU WANT TO REPLICATE

I have heard J. D. Greear say this many times and it has stuck with me: "What you celebrate, you replicate."[6] That simple phrase is incredibly important to keep in mind at any level of leadership but especially in the home. The things that we want to see manifested in our family should be the things we celebrate and praise the most.

We often celebrate when someone graduates from school or gets a promotion at work. Our families will go out to a restaurant to celebrate getting a good report card or scoring the game-winning goal. All of those things are amazing moments in life that mark progress or substantive memories. They are moments and milestones that ought to be celebrated.

Let us be certain that we celebrate moments and milestones in the faith with the same fervor. There are so many moments in our faith journey to be celebrated. All the while, God has kindly given us people that are close to us—who love us—that we have the blessing of celebrating with. Giving recognition to the God-ordained moments that happen in our lives allows us to testify to the grace of God.

You see this play out with Jesus and the demoniac in Mark 5. Jesus and the disciples had just crossed the Sea of Galilee to the country of the Gerasenes. As Jesus and His disciples got out of the boat, they came across a man who was demon-possessed and who was a torment to the people of the surrounding area. This man lived among the tombs, cut himself, and screamed out day and night. When Jesus encountered this man, He cast the demons out of him. The now healed man wanted to follow Jesus as one of His disciples, but Jesus turned him away and sent him home to his friends so that he could testify to what Jesus had done that day.

The man had a story of power and grace to tell, and Jesus wanted to be sure that the first people the man told were those whom he loved the most. Our first opportunity to celebrate the kindness and grace of God is with the people we love the most. Let us rejoice when God moves in the lives of the people we love.

Let us also rejoice when we see people move after the God they love. Let's celebrate the salvations, baptisms, mission trips, evangelistic opportunities, and even the small steps of Christlikeness we take. If there is anything worth celebrating, then share and rejoice in the work of God in the lives of His people.

Ministry and leadership happen at home before they happen anywhere else. Our chance to walk in gospel opportunities is dependent upon who we are and what we do when we are in the walls of our homes. The people we share our homes with are those who witness our sanctifying walk with Jesus. They are the people who are there to cheer us on as we learn endurance. The people under our roof deserve to receive the best we have to give while they watch us live for the Lord we love.

CHAPTER 8

MADE TO WITNESS

Then he said to his disciples, "The harvest is plentiful, but the laborers are few; therefore pray earnestly to the Lord of the harvest to send out laborers into his harvest."

MATTHEW 9:37-38

I grew up in the tiny town of Julian, North Carolina, which is nothing more than a dot in the center part of the state. Our "downtown" consisted of a gas station, a cemetery, a post office, and a milling company where many of the local farmers bought what they needed to run their farms. The mill should be the context clue that I grew up in a very rural area. Most people in our area were farmers or owned cattle. Those that did not have a farm at least had a vegetable garden. Julian is an agricultural locale through and through.

My neighbor across the road was one of the local farmers. He had about twenty-five acres of land where he raised cattle and grew an enormous vegetable garden that had about every vegetable you could grow in North Carolina. The first time I met him, he had come by our house to bring our family some of the surplus from his garden. I was only five years old at the time, but I thought being a farmer was the coolest job on the planet.

That day I had probably a hundred questions for him. In his kindness, he sat on our back porch and answered every single one of them. He never forgot that day and tried his best to teach me a little bit about farming over the years. He even gave me my first paying job as a teenager, helping him bale hay. I am sure it was quite the sight for everyone driving by his field to see my armless self picking up square bales of hay by the baling twine and putting them on the back of his trailer.

I will never forget showing up to his barn early one morning when we were getting ready to bale the hay in his field. He showed me both his tractors, his hay baler, and the rest of his equipment. There was not a single item in that barn that had been manufactured in my lifetime. One of his tractors, an old Ford, had to be at least forty years old. It was mostly blue and white with the occasional splash of rust in the paint. It was not the newest equipment, but he kept it well maintained and ready to go at a moment's notice.

That day left quite an impression on me as a young man. My neighbor did not need the best equipment to do what he needed to get done. He had what he needed, and he maintained it to meet his high standards. His preparation, even after all those years, paired with his sixty years of practical knowledge gave him what no new tractor ever could.

The lesson I learned about the benefits of preparedness and practical understanding lingered late into my teens and into adulthood. I was aware from an early age that I have many shortcomings when it comes to my calling in ministry. First off, I am not a people person by any stretch of the imagination. I get stressed out and frazzled in social situations if I do not prepare mentally in advance. Secondly, I am not a natural communicator. Communicating on any level, whether to small or large groups, is absolutely terrifying to me. I have to spend hours preparing to speak and preach just so I can put thoughts into a coherent form.

Those two weaknesses are not only hindrances to me in pastoral ministry but also when it comes to sharing the gospel with people in my everyday life. Due to my armlessness, I find myself in conversations with complete strangers on an almost daily basis. A routine trip to get gas or pick up an item at the grocery store will quickly morph into a conversation with curious strangers who want to know what a life without arms is really like.

Early on in my faith, I did not have the confidence or words to turn those conversations of curiosity into gospel conversations. I would feel the prompting of the Holy Spirit to turn the conversation into one about Jesus, but I felt like I did not have the words to say that would be meaningful to someone else. I was stuck in an evangelistic rut.

I stayed entrenched in that rut until I reached my freshman year of college and attended my first class: Personal Evangelism. That class did not give me a foolproof way to share the gospel with people nor did it point me to a foolproof gospel tract that I could share with others. But it awakened me to the gospel need of the world and the urgency of the hour. It gave me the nudge I needed to push past my perceived personal weaknesses and utilize every opportunity that came my way to share the gospel with others.

I wish I had a success story right out of the gates, but I struggled to share the gospel with people in one-on-one settings. I fumbled with my words and struggled to turn the conversation toward Jesus without it seeming harsh or disjointed. I made mistakes, but I was also learning. I was able to take what went on in each conversation and apply it to the next.

Now that I am eighteen years removed from my Personal Evangelism class (and even further removed from my neighbor's example of preparedness in farming), I can say that I try to share the gospel with someone personally at least once a week. I still have some trepidation about knowing what to say, and I am still uncomfortable putting myself out there, but I am doing what God has asked of me. I am seeking to be the one who sows the seed of the gospel like Jesus talks about in Matthew 13. It is not up to me to produce the growth of the gospel seed in the lives of others, but I am responsible to cast that gospel seed as I see the opportunity.

Now we will take some time to look at ways we can sow the gospel seed. This is not some sort of foolproof method to share the gospel. (If you are looking for that, I recommend the Three Circles method by Jimmy Scroggins.) This chapter focuses on being prepared for gospel-sharing opportunities and putting ourselves in positions to communicate the hope of the gospel to the people who need it.

LAY OUT YOUR TESTIMONY

I get asked to share my testimony with audiences all over the world: churches, schools, colleges, nonprofits, professional sports teams. When we share our testimonies, we audibly remind ourselves of the hope Jesus brought into our lives. I get to reflect on my broken life before I trusted Jesus as Lord as well as the new life, passions, and hope that I now have in Christ.

After sharing my testimony, people approach me with all sorts of questions and feedback, yet one common response I hear breaks my heart: "I wish I had a testimony like yours. I don't have a good testimony." There is no such thing as a "good testimony." Your testimony is the testament of the grace of God in your life. As Paul says, describing the effect of the grace of

God in his life, "But by the grace of God I am what I am, and his grace toward me was not in vain. On the contrary, I worked harder than any of them, though it was not I, but the grace of God that is with me" (1 Corinthians 15:10). Our testimony is our chance to share with others how the grace of God has changed our lives. I know I said that there is no such thing as a good or bad testimony, but there is a good *way* to share your testimony. There has to be a revealing of the grace and glory of God in our lives. A Christian testimony is our way of saying we know that God is who He says He is.

The trap that some people fall into when they are sharing their testimony is to make the account all about them. They share about their life before Christ: their sins, their failures, their hopelessness, or their emptiness. They lay out their laundry list of what they did before they knew Jesus as Lord and then abruptly end their testimony with how they came to confess Jesus as Lord. That is where they end and leave things there. A testimony needs more than that.

The testimony of someone who has been raised to walk in the newness of life (Romans 6:4) should spend some time telling about what Jesus has done beyond the salvation moment. What has changed in your life? What is present in your life now that was not before you were a Christian? What is God teaching you about Himself? The testimony of the Christian should spend a good amount of time recounting the grace that has come with being a part of God's adopted family.

I encourage you to think of your testimony as having three parts: your life before Christ, your life as you confessed Christ as Lord, and your life after Christ. You may not remember much of life before you confessed Christ, but at some point, you knew you needed a Savior. Others spent a significant time away from Jesus and have significant brokenness in their past.

Find a way to share that quickly without making your sin or yourself the main character of your testimony.

Then there came a time when you trusted Jesus as Lord and repented of your sinful past. Some of us can clearly remember where we were and what happened that brought us to that point. For others, that moment was more a gradual shift from living for themselves to living for Jesus. Whatever the case, this is the perfect point to share the gospel by laying out your helplessness as a sinner, Jesus dying on your behalf, and you confessing Him as Lord.

In any testimony, talk about the change God has brought into your life. This is the time to thank God for the new life that He has given you by adopting you as His child. Share the transformation, the hope, the joy, the wisdom, or whatever else you can think of that He has blessed you with. Take time to testify to the fact that He is who He says He is.

Think about how you would communicate those three parts to someone in a normal conversation and how to share your story quickly. Do not be ashamed of whatever is contained in your testimony. You are not telling *your* story—you are telling God's story of grace in your life. Have that story tucked away in the back of your mind so that it is ready to share whenever the opportunity presents itself.

BE READY TO SHARE THE
HOPE YOU HAVE

Now that we have our testimonies tucked away in the back of our brains, we need to ready ourselves to share that hope when the moment comes. Just as my old neighbor took great care to prepare himself to harvest his hay each year, so we should invest the same effort to prepare ourselves for the possibility of a gospel harvest in our everyday lives. This preparation is worth the effort. It is worth the eternal hope of a person you love or a person you just met.

The hard part comes from never truly knowing when a gospel opportunity will present itself. It can happen in a conversation with a good friend, or it can happen while you wait in line at Walmart. You should always be ready. Paul gives this command to the dispersed and persecuted church in 1 Peter 3:15: "But in your hearts honor Christ the Lord as holy, always being prepared to make a defense to anyone who asks you for a reason for the hope that is in you; yet do it with gentleness and respect." These people are under duress for their faith, and Peter pushes them to still share hope with those who hurt them.

It is crucial to recognize and emphasize sharing the "reason for the hope" that is in us. In our ever divided and bombastic culture, the natural defense our hearts want to give is how we are right and how someone else is wrong, especially when it comes to matters of politics or religion. It can be a divisive moment when we start to defend our rightness and their wrongness, but that is not what we are supposed to defend.

Give a defense for the hope that lives inside of you. Defense literally means "to give a reasoned or clear statement of." We always need to be ready to clearly tell others why we have hope and how they can have hope. That is the defense the believer needs to prepare for day in and day out.

Our preparation could be a simple prayer to begin our day: "God help me share my hope in you today." It could mean we mentally process our day in advance of getting it going. Where could there be gospel opportunities in the places that my feet will take me today? Those plans and possibilities may never manifest in a given day, but if we are not faithful to ready ourselves beforehand, we will miss out on those precious God-ordained gospel moments when they unfold before our eyes.

SHARE YOUR HURT

*Blessed be the God and Father of our Lord Jesus Christ, the
Father of mercies and God of all comfort, who comforts
us in all our affliction, so that we may be able to comfort
those who are in any affliction, with the comfort with
which we ourselves are comforted by God. For as we share
abundantly in Christ's sufferings, so through Christ we
share abundantly in comfort too.*

2 CORINTHIANS 1:3–5

The moments of suffering and trial that sweep through our lives
are usually the moments that capture the attention of those
closest to us. They want to be certain that we are fine. They
want to check in and see if there is anything that they can do.
Our seasons of affliction reveal the people who are truly our
friends when they willingly step into the darkness with us to
help us walk through whatever may come.

In those times of darkness, we can also be a true, loving
friend by sharing our hurts with the friends in our lives. As
the attention of our loved ones turns to us, we can reflect that
attention to Him. God can—and will—take your moments of
affliction and trial and use them as an opportunity for you to
share gospel hope with anyone willing to listen.

Although these dark days of hurt bring much pain for the
Christian, these are the days where the strength of God is
most clearly seen in our weakness. The times when we seem
to have little reveal the sustaining grace of God that bolsters
every corner of our lives. In our times of darkness, His light
in our lives shines all the more clearly. These moments trans-
form what we know about God into tangible lessons about His
comfort and grace.

We can share His comfort with those who need it the most. It is a comfort that spans our hurts and doubts. It is a comfort that can come from no other place than God. It is a life-altering comfort and hope that is meant to be a salve to you and a message of hope to all you are close with. Be willing to share both your hurt and your hope with the people you love.

LET PEOPLE WHO DO NOT KNOW JESUS INTO YOUR LIFE

Let me put this out there: you need to have people in your life who are not Christians. I realize that can open up a whole can of worms. People will justifiably point to 2 Corinthians 6:14: "Do not be unequally yoked with unbelievers. For what partnership has righteousness with lawlessness? Or what fellowship has light with darkness?"

We need some expositional precision while examining this text. Paul is pressing the Corinthian church to take great care as to who they are closely yoked with. Those who conflate their worldview with cultural lifestyle practices must be careful. The Christian cannot link the belief the world has about God to one's faith. Assuming culture in this way into one's faith will have disastrous consequences.

What Paul does not prohibit here is having friends who do not know Jesus as Lord. He tells us to exercise wisdom in how we relate to nonbelievers as well as being able to speak gracious words into their lives. Scripture says in Colossians 4:5–6, "Walk in wisdom toward outsiders, making the best use of the time. Let your speech always be gracious, seasoned with salt, so that you may know how you ought to answer each person."

The challenge here is to be wise with every minute we have. We need to be aware that every relationship and every conversation can be a vehicle by which the hope of the gospel can be shared. As we have seen by the spirit of the age we live in, the world is starved for hope, and the Christian has the only hope of the world. God can and will use you in the lives of those who do not know Jesus as long as you are willing.

In our culture today, unchurched people are willing to talk about faith. According to a Lifeway Research study, among those who are unchurched and not a Christian, 79 percent of those polled said they do not mind talking about a close friend's Christian faith. Of those in this study, 51 percent of them said the most effective means of them going to a church would be if a friend or family member invited them.[7]

Your relationships with those who do not know the hope of Jesus are meaningful. Who you invest in and love matters, so pour into the people in your life who do not know Jesus as Lord. You may be their one example of what Christ-centered living and hope actually look like.

BE KIND TO STRANGERS

Kindness seems like a benign or mundane aim for a person to have, but I do not think that is the case given the nature of our culture. It seems like many people are perched on the edge of exploding in anger at any moment. All they need is the right shove.

It reminds me of a YouTube channel my kids (and I) like a lot called Dude Perfect. Most of their videos feature wild trick shots using a football or a ping pong ball, but they also have a video series called "Stereotypes" where they point out the sort of people you would find at the gym, movie theater, or at the grocery store. In every one of these "Stereotype" videos they have a character called the "Rage Monster." If one thing goes wrong, this guy flies into a slapstick rage where he destroys everything in sight.

The people we come across are not on the precipice of being a Rage Monster, but they also aren't far away. We have all seen people treat one another terribly in a variety of ways. We have witnessed the spats people have on social media over their political beliefs and the name-calling fallout. We have seen the person behind the customer service desk at Target get blasted because someone's most recent purchase fell apart. We have heard the small group gossip at our local coffeehouse targeting a couple's recent marital problems.

We have all witnessed—and have been a part of—every one of those scenarios, and every one of those scenarios shame the name of Christ. There is no place for jerks in the kingdom of God. With effort and a little bit of prayer, we can be kind and patient toward others in high-stress situations. The new life that we have in Christ should express the kindness that Jesus has shown us.

"Be kind to one another, tenderhearted, forgiving one another, as God in Christ forgave you" (Ephesians 4:32). Kind and patient words are so countercultural that Christlike kindness extended to someone in a time when they deserve your personal wrath is bound to get attention. Love and kindness are the fruits of a kingdom that is rooted in Christ. The kindness of our King stands starkly against a world saturated in anger and strife. Allow the kind actions of Christ to be an avenue for you to share the powerful gospel of Christ.

SCATTER SEED WHERE GOD HAS SOVEREIGNLY PLANTED YOU

Jesus masterfully sums up the commandments of God in Matthew 22 when He says that the first and greatest commandment is to love God with all that we are. The second commandment is to love our neighbors just as we love ourselves.

Jesus elaborates in the parable of the good Samaritan that "neighbor" is a very broad category. Our neighbors do not have to look like us, talk like us, or vote like us in order for us to love them. We love our neighbors because they bear the Maker's image.

While we see that the biblical definition for a neighbor is a broad one, I do not think we should lose sight of the meaning of "neighbor" as one who lives near us. The church needs to be people who reach out and love those closest to them—whether that be relationally or geographically. God knew what He was doing when He sovereignly placed you at the address you call home.

He has set you among a field of people who need to see the Jesus you hold dear, but getting them to see Jesus is more difficult these days. Fifty years ago, we were a culture of front porch people. We knew our neighbors and their kids. We saw them out and about almost every day. These days we have moved our lives to the backyard and surrounded that yard with an eight-foot privacy fence. We have become more protective of our time and our families.

Christians have to be intentional about serving and loving our neighbors. It could be inviting our neighbors over for dinner or making them a plate of cookies on their birthday. It could be as unseen as pushing their trash cans up their driveway while they are at work or keeping an eye out for their house while they are on vacation.

Your neighbors are the people you live your life out with every day. They see your comings and goings. They see your backyard birthday parties and hear your yappy dog when the delivery guy drops something at your door. They know the minutiae of your life—so make sure they know about the Jesus you love.

KNOW THAT THE HOUR IS URGENT

*Go therefore and make disciples of all nations, baptizing them
in the name of the Father and of the Son and of the Holy
Spirit, teaching them to observe all that I have commanded
you. And behold, I am with you always, to the end of the age.*

MATTHEW 28:19-20

What turned the tide in my evangelistic life was realizing the
gospel need of the world and the urgency to get the gospel to
people. There is no escaping the promise that apart from the
saving work of Christ, people will die and spend an eternity
separated from God in hell. There is no changing our eternal
destination once we pass from this life to the next. Our eter-
nities are finalized on this side of death, but we have no idea
when that moment comes on the timeline.

The people who you love need to know Jesus as Lord in
order to be saved, and God has placed you in their lives to
do just that. The hope of Jesus should not be something we
keep putting off until it just "comes up" one day. The Great
Commission should be in the forefront of our minds because
the time is coming when we will not have the chance to tell
those we love about our God.

"We must work the works of him who sent me while it is
day; night is coming, when no one can work. As long as I am
in the world, I am the light of the world" (John 9:4–5). Jesus
speaks this command right before healing a man who has been
blind his entire life. The blind man is about to have the scope
of his life changed forever in a miraculous event, but Jesus
wanted to hammer home the point that there are many more
spiritually blind who need the saving work of who He is—the
light of the world.

Whether we find ourselves in times of joy or in the doldrums, there is a gospel need around you right now. The great lie of Satan is that there is no rush to get the gospel to the people whose lives orbit yours. Satan wants your silence. Christ has called you to go while you can because there is a day not far off where you will not be able to.

Go now. Night is coming.

The Great Commission cannot be a pursuit for only the Christians who claim ministry as their profession. This is a command for all believers starting right now. The need is great; the hour is short. The only hope for the world now and for the long run is for every believer to go and tell of Jesus's gospel.

CHAPTER 9

MADE TO BUILD BRICK BY BRICK

*Then Jesus told his disciples, "If anyone would come after
me, let him deny himself and take up his cross and follow
me. For whoever would save his life will lose it, but whoever
loses his life for my sake will find it.*

MATTHEW 16:24-25

When I submitted to Jesus as Lord as a fifteen-year-old, I
would be the first to tell you that I was a "church kid."
I had spent my entire life up to that point going to church
every week. I went to Sunday morning worship, youth group
on Wednesday nights, and even sang in the youth choir. If the
church doors were open, my family was typically there.

All those events and worship services added up to countless
hours spent at church. I knew what to do when I was at church,
but I had no idea how to live as a Christian once I walked out
the doors on Sunday. I had no frame of reference for how to
find my way out of my spiritual cluelessness until a man tapped
me on the shoulder one day at church. His name was Alex,
and I only vaguely knew him at the time. He was a member of
my church and had preached a couple of times at our Sunday

morning services. I didn't know it then, but Alex was a prolific author of Christian books on theology and apologetics and had taught at a couple of Christian colleges.

Alex tapped me on the shoulder to ask if anyone in my life was discipling me. I told him honestly that I didn't even know what that word meant, much less whether anyone was helping me to disciple. I remember him telling me that discipleship is just one Christian bringing another Christian along on their life journey so they can know what it looks like to follow Jesus. He asked if I would like to be discipled by him, to which I quickly answered yes, and he told me to meet him at a local diner for breakfast the following Saturday.

For that Saturday and many more to come, Alex and I would meet at that diner to eat, talk, laugh, and pray. We talked about a lot of things over the span of those breakfasts. He shared his testimony with me, and I shared my testimony with him. I asked him all the questions about life and faith that I could think of. He taught me about the reliability of Scripture and the historical proofs of the resurrection. Alex showed me how he loved and served his wife, and he talked to me about how he tried to love his critics well even when they didn't love him. We spent time encouraging each other and praying for each other.

I am so grateful to God for His grace in giving me a relationship with Alex in those very early, clueless days in my faith. He was my greatest encourager and the mentor I needed for the days that lay ahead of me. He was the first of many men over the next twenty years who would walk alongside me so I could grow in my faith and follow Jesus with every part of my being. Those relationships played a vital role in me enduring, in running the race, in both my faith and ministry.

Those relationships also directly affected how I do ministry, especially in how I led the students that I was responsible for in my days as a student pastor. I poured just as much time into intentional one-on-one discipleship in my ministry as I did any other aspect of my role as a student pastor. Preparing and preaching sermons is incredibly important, but so is imparting what a life in Christ looks like away from the church building.

Grabbing hold of a life of following Jesus may mean someone grabbing hold of you to show you what lays ahead, just like Alex did with me. It is also what Barnabas did with Paul in Acts 11. We see the conversion of Paul in Acts 9, and almost immediately Paul begins to teach everyone he encounters about the risen Messiah he just met on the road to Damascus. Yet, that teaching began to elicit criticism and persecution that was aimed directly at Paul. Eventually, Paul's opposition grew to the level of death threats, which caused the church leaders to send Paul to Tarsus for his own safety.

Paul remained there for an untold amount of time until Barnabas went to Tarsus to bring Paul along to serve the church at Antioch. The two men stayed in Antioch for a year as they encouraged the church together. Acts 11 does not explicitly say that Barnabas discipled Paul, but Barnabas's track record shows what he was up to. He consistently encouraged the church and pressed them to continually follow after the purpose and mission of God. This was the man that God sovereignly placed Paul with for twelve months.

Barnabas was precisely the person that a baby-faithed Paul needed. Paul needed someone to show him the ropes of ministry and how to love and lead as an elder. He needed the chance to lead and teach under the watchful eye of a person who had been down the road he was heading down. He needed encouragement in advance of the tidal wave of affliction he was about to face.

The church today is different than it was two thousand years ago in Paul and Barnabas's day. But we still need people who will encourage us and guide us as we learn to endure in faith. We need loving people whom we can imitate and learn from. We, as the church, need to actively seek out others to disciple, just like Barnabas did with Paul. Let us look at some ways we can integrate Christ-imitating relationships into our lives so that we may grow in Christ and walk in the mission of Christ even when we are off church grounds.

FIND SOMEONE TO IMITATE

All of us need people to follow after who are well into their run of faith. No matter where we are in our spiritual walk—new believer, believer for a few decades, or an elder—we need people in our lives who can love and lead us through whatever may come our way. One of the best ways we learn is through imitation—our ability to observe and repeat the action or behavior we have seen.

We are especially adept at this as children. My two kids are always watching and learning. They love to glean information from books and videos, and they love to do and say what they hear from me and their mom. As they have watched and imitated me through the years, they have picked up some rather unique talents. There will be times at the dinner table when I glance over at my daughter and see that she is eating a hot dog with her toes. Obviously she has been taking mental notes from her daddy on that one.

We learn best when we can watch and repeat. This is also true when it comes to our faith in Christ. Great benefits come through being taught audibly or through a book, but also great benefits and comfort can come from watching others and following what they have done. Paul tells the Corinthian church, "Be imitators of me, as I am of Christ" (1 Corinthians 11:1). After telling the church that they ought to do everything in their lives to the glory of God, he then points to his own life as a frame of reference. The church needs more people who love Jesus with their everything to lead others in how we can do the same.

We all need people whom we can imitate as they follow their Lord. We need people who can point us to places of spiritual nourishment while also helping us to avoid the pitfalls of life. It does not matter where we are on the timeline of faith, we all need people we can look to that can challenge us to love Jesus more and serve Him well.

I encourage you to find someone in your life who can bring you along on their life journey so you can know what it looks like to follow Jesus. Simply ask someone to show you how they love and live for Jesus—that's the essence of discipleship. Don't feel intimidated as you ask. It is a great encouragement to people for someone to recognize their faith and to be asked how to get there. Find someone to follow who is following Jesus. That is how we grow and gain ground in this long faith journey.

INVITE SOMEONE ALONG ON YOUR FAITH JOURNEY

Just as we should be seeking out someone to imitate, so we should be looking for someone who can imitate us. Like we saw at the end of the last chapter, the Great Commission is the command of all believers. Those who follow Jesus are expected to show others the new, amazing life hope that they have in the Savior: "Him we proclaim, warning everyone and teaching everyone with all wisdom, that we may present everyone mature in Christ. For this I toil, struggling with all his energy that he powerfully works within me" (Colossians 1:28–29).

The Christian is deeply passionate about sharing the gospel with those who do not know Jesus as Lord, but that isn't where the Christian stops. We are people who introduce others to

Jesus, but we also walk hand in hand with those who have submitted to Jesus as Lord so they can be shown all that the Christian life entails. Christian maturity comes as a person is poured into, and the picture of someone who is mature in Christ is the person willing to share their life for the maturation of others.

It is a hard step for many of us to take. It was for me. I am a naturally quiet and introverted person. I do not want to be in a room with another person, much less have my life be an open book for someone else to peer into. In my early days of faith, I was uncomfortable with putting myself out there. However, the mission of God matters more than my comfort and convenience.

Think through the people you know in your neighborhood, church, school, or office building. Who knows Jesus as their Lord and Savior? How many of those people need a meaningful faith relationship? I daresay every Christian needs someone in their life who they can talk to about the most important aspect of their life: their faith.

Find a person and ask if they want discipleship to be a consistent part of their life. You don't have to specifically ask them, "Do you want to be discipled?" You could organize meeting once a week over coffee or lunch to talk about what Jesus is doing in your life. It might mean studying a book of the Bible with one of your friends. Whatever it looks like, your faith was never meant to happen in isolation. Live out your pursuit of Jesus and invite other people along. This is a powerful way that we can watch, imitate, and grow in grace.

DO NOT STOP GROWING

One of the most amazing and challenging aspects of our growth in Christ is that we are never done growing. From the moment we trust in Jesus as Lord to the moment we take our final breath, there is more to know and more to tell about the God we trust. There is never a point where we can say, "I have finally made it! I am a totally mature Christian." We grow until we're gone. That is a motto I think the apostle Paul would have gotten behind. He even takes that idea further in Philippians 3:

> Not that I have already obtained this or am already perfect, but I press on to make it my own, because Christ Jesus has made me his own. Brothers, I do not consider that I have made it my own. But one thing I do: forgetting what lies behind and straining forward to what lies ahead, I press on toward the goal for the prize of the upward call of God in Christ Jesus. Let those of us who are mature think this way, and if in anything you think otherwise, God will reveal that also to you. (Philippians 3:12–15)

Take a step back and think of all Paul did in his life up to the point of writing the book of Philippians. God led Paul on a missionary journey that helped to establish the Gentile church across the Mediterranean. God used and continued to use the hand of Paul to write the bulk of what would become the New Testament. God used the teaching of Paul in such a powerful way that both the Jewish and Roman governments felt their power was threatened.

It is *that guy* who says in Philippians 3 that he has not gotten there yet. He has not made it. He is not done growing. He has more to grow in, and he has more to do for the King he lives his life for. He is going to live in such a way that he will strain toward the call God has for him until the moment he passes into eternity and faith becomes sight. Paul was not going to stop until Jesus told him, "Well done, good and faithful servant."

Yet, this is not just Paul living out his amazing faith journey; this is the expectation for all who call on Jesus as Lord. In Philippians 3 it says, "Let those of us who are mature think this way." Christian maturity produces the realization of how much more is left to go in our lives of faith. We are never done, and we have so much ahead of us.

That is why it is so important for us to not stop growing in grace. Continually feed yourself with the nourishment that is out there in the world. Fill your daily life with the meat of the Word of God. Read from the wealth of books that are available and listen to the multitude of sermon archives and church livestreams that are available online. We have more access to the gospel truth than at any other time in human history. Do not waste that! Do not stop growing! God has so much in store for you if you are faithful to seek Him.

HAVE SOMEONE WHO CAN CALL YOU OUT

The ear that listens to life-giving reproof
will dwell among the wise.
Whoever ignores instruction despises himself,
but he who listens to reproof gains intelligence.
PROVERBS 15:31-32

Human nature bristles against accountability. None of us wants to be told we have missed the mark. When it comes to our Christian walk, none of us wants to be told that we are living in disobedience to the Creator and Sustainer of the world. We are all content to never have a conversation like that—which is the problem.

Our fallen nature would be perfectly fine with never having our sins exposed and uprooted, but there are times when we need that. We need other people who love us to shine a light on the parts of our lives where we are walking in disobedience against God. We cannot be the only people who look over the deeds of our hearts. We are the worst judges of ourselves. As we see in Jeremiah 17:9, "the heart is deceitful above all things, and desperately sick; who can understand it?"

Your heart is skillful at lying to you. You need someone in your life who can lovingly rebuke you in the midst of your sin. Having a person like that in your life is one of the healthiest and wisest decisions a believer can make.

It is up to us to invite that sort of reproof into our lives. When it comes to sin in the lives of others, many people stay quiet because they feel like that is none of their business. We should go to the people in our lives who love us the most—spouse, relative, best friend—and give them a green light to point out the sins that creep in the recesses of our hearts. It is then our job to do something about it. We need to listen to Christ-honoring rebuke, knowing that tough love allows us to continue to walk on the path of faith with sure footing.

EDIFY THE GOOD GIFTS IN OTHERS

If there was one thing I was convinced of in my young faith, it was that I was *never* going to be a pastor. As I have mentioned before, I was a recovering people hater in my youth. I did not enjoy being around a couple of people, much less imagining myself preaching to a crowd of people. I was convinced that everything you needed to be a pastor was everything I did not have.

That was the case for the first few months of my faith. I doubted everything about the gifts and the calling of God in my life until God kept placing encouraging people in front of me. First and foremost was my mom, Emily Ritchie. From my infancy, she felt that God had big things in store for me and that He was going to use me to take the gospel globally. She thought that from day one of my life, and she was persistent in letting me know that in my teens.

I also had an associate pastor at my church named Marty Tobin. He is not overly wordy, and when he speaks it is almost always wise and insightful. I will never forget crossing paths with him at church one day when he told me that he felt like God had gifted and called me to be a preacher. The comment was totally unprompted; he just felt the Lord wanted me to hear that.

That happened probably three or four more times over the next few months with different people, which led me to wonder if everyone else was seeing something I was missing—which was exactly the case. I was blind to God's gifts and calling because of my fear and insecurity. I could not see the very clear fruit that God had cultivated in my life, but everyone else could. The encouragement and edification from other people pushed me to prayerfully submit to the calling and to use the gifts God has given me.

We should not seek to flatter and puff up those around us, but we also should be faithful to affirm what we see. As the author of Hebrews implores, "But exhort one another every day, as long as it is called 'today,' that none of you may be hardened by the deceitfulness of sin" (Hebrews 3:13). We need to faithfully affirm the gifts of God in the lives of others because there are many who do not see the grace of God in their lives that you do. When you see the gifts of God in the lives of others, point them out. Affirm them—not for your good but for theirs.

SUFFER WELL

If there is an overlooked promise in Scripture, it is Jesus's promise in John 16:33: "I have said these things to you, that in me you may have peace. In the world you will have tribulation. But take heart; I have overcome the world." We will suffer as we follow Him. Believers must ready their hearts for the cost of discipleship: trusting Jesus as Lord does not dismiss the Christian from suffering; it guarantees it.

Discipleship is filled with trials and tribulation, but that is not a mistake on God's part. The trials of this world reveal that things are not as they were in the beginning. At the dawn of creation, the world was free from toil and death. When Adam and Eve chose the fruit over their Father, they brought on the consequences of frustration, death, and separation from God with one sinful act. However, God in His kindness proclaims hope even as He lays out the consequences of sin. Hope was on the way—a man would crush the work of Satan with His foot.

This crushing of the serpent would bruise the heel of the Savior, yet because of His wounding, we would taste and see the grace of God. Ever since that moment in the garden of Eden, God has been present with us in our suffering. And He is not only present but is redeeming and working in our suffering so that His will may be done. The moments of suffering remind us of whom we have entrusted our lives to: "But we have this treasure in jars of clay, to show that the surpassing power belongs to God and not to us" (2 Corinthians 4:7).

In our weakness His power is fully made known (2 Corinthians 12:9). Just as we saw in the chapter on evangelism, God can use our suffering as a way to share His gospel. Suffering also allows the believer to see the character of God more clearly. Our trials produce steadfastness (James 1:3) and refine and strengthen our faith (1 Peter 1:6–7).

Following after Christ will bring us suffering, but it is our suffering that will deepen our faith in Christ. Do not fear when suffering comes. God is still present with you through it. He loves you, He is for you, and He is working in your life. Know that suffering is coming, but remember it can help you grow as a disciple even as you struggle and fight through it. Our faith will grow and be bolstered as we press on through hardship.

PREACH THE GOSPEL TO YOURSELF

One of the most life-giving acts for Christians is to remind themselves of the good news of the gospel. This world is saturated with bad news. We do not need to look far for something that can discourage our hearts, but praise God that the best news to ever grace the planet is also close at hand: "For God so loved the world, that he gave his only Son, that whoever believes in him should not perish but have eternal life. For God did not send his Son into the world to condemn the world, but in order that the world might be saved through him" (John 3:16–17).

God loved the world to the degree that He sacrificed His son to buy His children out of the slavery to fear of sin and death. He did not send an army to the world to condemn it and wipe it out for its sinful acts. He sent a Savior to deliver humanity from a purposeless life and a hopeless eternity. That gospel is fantastic news to those of us who were once enemies of God but are now called adopted sons and daughters.

That great news cannot be preached frequently enough or loudly enough. The hope-filled gospel is not only an introduction to the faith for the believer, but it is also the sustaining grace for the Christian: "Now I would remind you, brothers, of the gospel I preached to you, which you received, in which you stand, and by which you are being saved, if you hold fast

to the word I preached to you—unless you believed in vain"
(1 Corinthians 15:1–2).

The gospel is the means by which I am saved, but it is also
the means by which I stand right now. It is not just our ground-
floor entry to the Christian faith; it is the supporting and sustaining power that spans the length of the believer's life. For us
to grow as disciples of Jesus we must remind ourselves of how
a good and glorious God has saved and is using people like us.
To God be the glory in all my days!

Discipleship is the long grind of the Christian faith. It is a
process that begins at salvation and ends when we step into
glory—everywhere in between is discipleship being played out.
It is a process that is never finished and is not meant to happen
in isolation. It is one of the greatest gifts that God has granted
us as we endure in faith. We get to follow the Lord we love
shoulder to shoulder with those who claim the same. May we
all embrace the winding road that is discipleship, knowing that
the Master we follow will not let it be in vain.

CASE STUDY

JOSEPH

WADING THROUGH SUFFERING

And the patriarchs, jealous of Joseph, sold him into Egypt; but God was with him and rescued him out of all his afflictions and gave him favor and wisdom before Pharaoh, king of Egypt, who made him ruler over Egypt and over all his household.

ACTS 7:9–10

The second Sunday of January 2020 was an eerie foretaste of the year to come. I had been asked by my good friend David McKinley to preach at his church, Warren Baptist Church, in Augusta, Georgia. He was taking some much-needed time off to spend with his family, and I was happy to fill in for him in his absence. This was not anything out of the ordinary because I fill in for pastors during their time away from their churches quite often.

But as soon as I walked into church that morning, my voice felt scratchy and weak, which is a bit of a problem for someone about to do nothing but talk for the next four hours. I grabbed a water and some cough drops out of my backpack and jumped into preaching the first service that morning. I managed to croak through without any issues.

The next service was the main service. The sanctuary was packed with congregants that morning. I took to the pulpit after the offertory and started my sermon. As I preach, I am not normally tied to my notes. I like to look around the sanctuary and make eye contact with people. I just happened to be scanning the balcony when I saw a pregnant woman throw up and collapse right in the middle of the sermon.

Immediately people were in a panic and someone shouted, "Is there a doctor?" It happened so fast I barely knew what to do. This was not my home church, so I had no idea what the protocol was for something like this, but within thirty seconds, the church's safety team circled around her and was assessing the situation.

At this point, there was no way I could keep going with the sermon. I stopped the sermon, and we spent the next few minutes in corporate prayer for this woman and her baby. By the time we had wrapped up our prayer time, she had been placed in an ambulance and taken to a local hospital. By the end of the service we had heard that she was in good condition and recovering from dehydration.

Once the service had finished, I slipped back to the church lobby to meet people and sign copies of my biography, *My Affliction for His Glory*. I got to meet a lot of amazing people that day, but one person stood out among the rest. His name was Trey, and he was an eight-year-old boy born without arms or legs. It would be safe to say we had a lot in common, and we hit it off immediately. I sat with Trey on the floor for a while as we talked about adaptations we both had to make in life, how we dealt with curious people, and how school was going. I laid my feet on Trey before we were finished and prayed for him and God's plan for his life.

As we got ready to leave, I spoke with the woman who had brought him to church that day. She made direct eye contact with me and said, "Don't stop what you're doing. God is using you in more ways than you can imagine." With that, she picked up Trey and they left. I was encouraged by her words and went back to meeting the last few people in the lobby.

In the next fifteen minutes, I had two more people who told me, "Don't quit what you're doing." At this point I realized God was trying to tell me something, but I had no idea what it could be. I loved what I was able to do as an evangelist and speaker. God was clearly opening doors for me, and we were watching tremendous amounts of spiritual fruit being produced from God's work in this ministry He had given me. I had zero desire to quit what I was doing.

Barely sixty days later, the state of North Carolina went into a stay-at-home order. Church doors shut and large gatherings were banned. My jam-packed ministry schedule was suddenly shot to pieces, and overnight our single-income family went to a zero-income family. I sat at home from March to July, watching cancellation after cancellation pour into my inbox. We began to wonder how we were going to pay the mortgage or feed our family. Our situation was getting desperate.

This was not what I had planned for 2020 at all. My wife Heather and I started to pray. We prayed for the favor of God. We prayed for those who were sick with COVID-19. We prayed for wisdom as to whether God wanted me to continue in a ministry that I could not do given the gathering restrictions in many states. As we prayed for weeks on end, the words from the church lobby kept ringing in my ears: "Don't stop what you're doing."

It was clear to us that we were to continue in this season of ministry. Things were incredibly difficult, but God provided for us in that difficult time. God had a plan for the future and God also had a plan for my time at home away from my ministry. In our family's suffering, we knew that God was at work.

Suffering has the power both to wreck lives and strengthen faith. In suffering, we hear the groaning of creation but we also see the power of God made known in our weakness. The suffering of humanity and the sovereignty of God are not divorced from one another. In fact, as we are about to see in the life of Joseph, suffering can be how the plans of God are executed. Let us look at the suffering of Joseph to glean some truths of how we can press on through the grueling times we face in our faith.

SMALL BEGINNINGS CAN
HAVE MAJOR IMPACTS

Then Pharaoh sent and called Joseph, and they quickly brought him out of the pit. And when he had shaved himself and changed his clothes, he came in before Pharaoh.

GENESIS 41:14

It would be fair to describe the life of Joseph as a roller coaster at this point. He went from favored son to slave. From slave to having authority over the house of one of Pharaoh's officers. From authority to a prison cell. From a prison cell to serving one of the most powerful men in the world by interpreting his dreams.

Through the ups and downs in Joseph's life, he remained a respectable man who worked really hard in everything. Hard work is what got him noticed by Potiphar. His willingness to serve anyone afforded him the chance to interpret the dreams of Pharaoh's cupbearer while they were both in prison. The same cupbearer recommended Joseph and his dream-interpreting skills to the leader of Egypt. Joseph's willingness to take the next faithful step led him into new roles time after time.

When life takes a significant detour and our plans fail, it is human nature to want to quit. Why should we bother with being persistent when all we do is fail? This is a natural reaction to trial and failure, but God has more in store for you and your life. Even in the seasons of life that seem like a total grind, God sees what you are doing. He sees your faithfulness with the little He has given you, and He desires to entrust you with more.

If it seems as if you are starting off on the bottom rung of the ladder in life, or if your life has been totally reset by the afflictions that have come your way, do not stop. Do not quit chasing after the things God has called you to. God made you for more than just quitting. He has given you opportunities—even if they are small—to glorify Him with what you have. Capitalize on those small beginnings knowing that God sees you and has more coming for you if you are faithful with what you have before you.

PEOPLE WHO LOVE YOU WILL WOUND YOU

They saw him from afar, and before he came near to them they conspired against him to kill him. They said to one another, "Here comes this dreamer. Come now, let us kill him and throw him into one of the pits. Then we will say that a fierce animal has devoured him, and we will see what will become of his dreams."

GENESIS 37:18-20

Joseph had many brothers who were very jealous of him and angry toward him. Joseph had a few dreams where his entire family was bowing down before him. Once Joseph shared these dreams with his brothers, he enraged them even more. In the midst of their anger, the brothers sought an opportunity to be rid of him once and for all.

Before they could murder Joseph, one of the brothers named Reuben stepped in to save Joseph from this plot by encouraging the other brothers not to kill him but to throw Joseph in a pit. The brothers went with Reuben's plan, and Reuben hoped he could rescue Joseph from the pit while the other brothers were preoccupied. However, Reuben's plan fell through when the brothers saw a group of traders passing by. They got rid of Joseph by selling him into slavery.

Joseph's own flesh and blood sold him into a life of hardship because of their jealousy and hatred. His story of betrayal is mirrored by the betrayal that Jesus suffered from Judas. Jesus's own disciple who had just broken bread with Him at the Last Supper sold Him out to the authorities for thirty pieces of silver.

It does not matter if you are an Old Testament witness like Joseph or the Savior of the world like Jesus—people are going to hurt you. They are going to betray you or slander you. In a moment of weakness, they might seek the worst for you and the best for them. The cost of living with broken, fallen, and sinful people is that they will do broken, fallen, and sinful things to you.

The hard part about being in relationship with others is they will eventually fall short of the expectations of love and kindness we have for them. We do not anticipate the wounding that comes from our friends, family, and even church members—but it will come eventually. We must prepare our hearts for the possibility of taking on hurt from within our own camp because, as we will see here in a minute with Joseph, we also have the opportunity to extend forgiveness to those who wound us.

SUFFERING COMES EVEN WHEN
WE DO THE RIGHT THINGS

*But one day, when he went into the house to do his work
and none of the men of the house was there in the house, she
caught him by his garment, saying, "Lie with me." But he left
his garment in her hand and fled and got out of the house.*

GENESIS 39:11-12

The favor of God remains on Joseph even when he is sent down
to Egypt as a slave. In his time there, Joseph earns the respect
of an officer of Pharaoh named Potiphar. Potiphar notes the
abilities and successes Joseph has at almost every turn. Potiphar
quickly promotes the slave Joseph to run everything that goes
on in his home.

However, Potiphar was not the only person drawn to Joseph.
Potiphar's wife took note of how attractive Joseph was. When
she saw her opportunity, she attempted to seduce him, but
to no avail. Joseph fled the house in an attempt to escape her
grasp. Even though he tried his best to pursue righteousness
in the moment, Potiphar's wife lied about Joseph's actions and
had him put in prison for something he never did.

Joseph had been betrayed by his own flesh and blood and
now had to deal with being imprisoned for doing the right
thing. That is something all of us can relate to on a basic level.
We have tried to be kind to someone else only to have it blow
up in our faces. We have tried to share the hope of the gospel
with someone we love only to be given the cold shoulder for
wanting to share the greatest news of the world. It can leave a
bad taste in your mouth to try to seek the best for others only
to have it hurt you.

God is not unaware of your actions or your heart. He knows what you are trying to do, and He wants you to keep going. He does not want you to grow weary of seeking righteousness in all you do. As Peter reminds the dispersed church in 1 Peter 3:14, "But even if you should suffer for righteousness' sake, you will be blessed. Have no fear of them, nor be troubled."

Peter is writing to the church that fled their homes because of persecution. In trying to live out their faith, the church was pushed out from the communities they had planted roots in. The promise here is that God not only sees the faith lived out by His people, but He will bless them for their endurance. The gospel seeds sown in trial are not lost. Suffering is well worth enduring for both our hearts and for those who bring the suffering upon us. The way we suffer and love well towards our persecutors speaks the power of God to them, even without words. All is not lost when we have to suffer for our faith. As we will see in the life of Joseph, God blesses His servant for his faithfulness.

GOD IS SOVEREIGN IN YOUR SUFFERING

And now do not be distressed or angry with yourselves because you sold me here, for God sent me before you to preserve life.
GENESIS 45:5

Joseph continued his ascent in Egypt by being promoted to governor of all of Egypt. Famine had swept through the land, but thanks to Joseph's interpretation of Pharaoh's dreams, he was able to prepare the nation in advance. Egypt had stored food while the surrounding nations had not. Soon, these neighboring nations began to go to Egypt to ask for food.

Just as so many others had, Joseph's brothers came to Egypt to find food for their family. In this moment Joseph came face to face with his brothers for the first time since they had betrayed him. Joseph had every bit of power and authority to exact revenge on his brothers, but he withheld from doing it. Not only did he hold back vengeance, but he used it as an opportunity to praise God. What the brothers were doing in sin, God was using to preserve His chosen people. God used one of the worst moments of Joseph's life to be a working piece of His sovereign plan.

It is not that God turned the choice of Joseph's brothers into a good thing. It is that God's means of saving both Joseph and his brothers was their betrayal of him. God used the lies of Potiphar's wife to put Joseph in prison with members of Pharaoh's service. Those lies put him in a position to stand before Pharaoh to interpret his dreams. God did not err and was not absent in Joseph's suffering; He was orchestrating it.

Some of us may cringe at the thought of God being sovereign in our suffering, but that is the best news in regard to our fate. God's sovereign work means that our suffering is not accidental. God did not mess up or let a moment escape. His grasp shows that our lives are not some culmination of random moments. The great news of God's sovereign work is that we are a part of His plan for His purpose. We are not tied to the ebb and flow of happenstance; we are living in the midst of a global gospel plan.

Do not fear when suffering comes. God is not distant but present and at work. Be encouraged, for the worst of what life has to offer will still be used for the good and the glory of God who is working through both the blessings and hardships we face in this life.

GOD'S PLANS EXCEED OURS

Joseph was thirty years old when he entered the service of Pharaoh king of Egypt. And Joseph went out from the presence of Pharaoh and went through all the land of Egypt. During the seven plentiful years the earth produced abundantly, and he gathered up all the food of these seven years, which occurred in the land of Egypt, and put the food in the cities. He put in every city the food from the fields around it. And Joseph stored up grain in great abundance, like the sand of the sea, until he ceased to measure it, for it could not be measured.

GENESIS 41:46–49

I doubt Joseph could have imagined that the story arc of his life would go from pit to prison to palace, but that is what God had in store for him. Joseph's story is cinematic with its rags-to-riches story line. Yet, this plan and story go far beyond Joseph as a main character.

This story has a gospel thread that runs right through the middle of it. God made a promise that a descendant of Adam would be the prophesied snake crusher of Genesis 3. From that chapter on, Scripture contains God's protection and preservation of the line of the descendants from the first Adam to the second Adam. God raising up Joseph to allow for provision of food for His promised people is a part of the greater gospel plan.

The great and glorious news for those of us in Christ is that we are a part of a plan that is so much greater than our own stories. For believers, the story of our lives fits into the great gospel arc that goes from the creation of humanity to the return of Christ. God is weaving our lives and stories into the grand plan of His mission. He is working something in us and through us that is far greater than us: "Now to him who is able to do far more abundantly than all that we ask or think, according to the power at work within us, to him be glory in the church and in Christ Jesus throughout all generations, forever and ever. Amen" (Ephesians 3:20–21).

We all want to be loved and for our lives to matter, and God accomplishes just that in the gospel. He fulfills those longings through our adoption as children and in our sending out as disciples. His love of us extends far past the love our earthly relationships could ever bring. His purpose for us to be disciples who make disciples is a mission that not only impacts the world but reverberates into eternity.

God is doing things in your life and through your life that you cannot fathom. The full impact of our lives submitted to Him cannot be fully calculated until we are in eternity. His grand plan is greater than ours—plain and simple. Trust His plan and know that you have placed yourself in the very center of God restoring all things unto Himself, and He is sewing your story into the grand tapestry of that glory.

Living our lives in view of eternity means we have to trust God's grand gospel plan even when we cannot see what is next. Living out the plans of God in our lives certainly means we will be met with suffering, but that is not a surprise to God. He is at work, even in your pain, so that you may trust Him more fully and the world may see Him in you wholly. We overcome the suffering of this life because we know the best is yet to come. We know that something is at work that we cannot yet fully see. We press on and we look up knowing our God will bring about a good that even our wildest imaginings cannot comprehend.

CHAPTER 10

WAITING WELL

Behold, as the eyes of servants
look to the hand of their master,
as the eyes of a maidservant
to the hand of her mistress,
so our eyes look to the LORD our God,
till he has mercy upon us.

PSALM 123:2

How can I keep with the tasks of everyday life while also pursuing Christ when I feel like all I do is fall behind? How can God be good—or even faithful—when His promises of love and power haven't come through yet? These questions are the cloud that weighs on us while we try to do the right things over the long haul. It can be a downright war on our spirit as we wait on the movement of God.

Few of us desire to grow in patience because that requires exercising patience to see it grow. We must wait, hope, and watch while the world swirls around us. Our fear is that we will get left behind as we wait. Left behind in our growth, left behind by the people we love, and left behind by God. It is incredibly hard to keep pressing forward when we feel as if we are stuck in neutral.

One of the most common questions people ask me is: "What is the hardest thing you had to learn to do with your feet?" While there are several difficult tasks I have had to learn to do, there is one thing that stands out among them all: learning to write. The hardship on the front end was that I had no one to model. Everyone I knew wrote with their hands, so I had no one to coach me through what I was trying to do. There was lots of trial and error just trying to learn how to hold a crayon or pencil with my feet.

The main difficulty I had in learning how to write was more biomechanical than anything. Writing with hands offers a lot of advantages: thumb, wrist, and natural grip strength. Writing with my feet offered none of those advantages. In the early days of first grade, I tried to write at a normal desk like all the other kids did, but that was a failure as well. Sitting at a normal desk placed my feet well above my hips for significant amounts of time, causing them to fall asleep.

Once we corrected that issue by having me sit in front of a lowered desk—which put my hips and feet at an even height—I was able to attempt writing for more than fifteen minutes at a time. However, my legs and feet were not able to handle the load I was putting on them. After about thirty minutes of simple writing, my feet and legs would lock up from painful leg cramps. Those cramps would stop me dead in my tracks, and I would not be able to complete the given assignment.

Those halfway done assignments started to stack up, and I fell behind the rest of my class. That eventually led to me having my desk put in the corner of the classroom, away from all my friends, so I could finish my assignments at my own pace. If I fell much more behind the class, I would have to be placed in an independent study learning environment until I caught up. This had to be one of the most isolating experiences of my time at school.

It was devastating to watch my classmates do writing assignments in one-third the time that it took me. I felt like such a failure when I had to stop writing to massage the cramps out of my feet and legs. I just needed my legs to catch up to what my mind wanted to do, but I was trapped in this situation until my muscles could adapt.

By Christmas break of my first-grade year, I had strengthened my leg muscles to the point where I could write for extended periods of time without issue. I had made up all my assignments and now had my desk back with the rest of my class. It was an absolutely brutal four months for me to get there, but I could be a normal first-grader again. Well, as normal as an armless kid can feasibly be.

Waiting on what lies ahead can be the hardest part of enduring the long run of faith. Whether it is waiting on an answer from the Lord or waiting for a season of painful darkness to pass, the war that goes on in our waiting can be brutal. So how can we press forward when we do not know what is next? How can we put one foot in front of the other when we are exhausted from the path we have already walked? Let's look at some rhythms we can pursue that will give us the strength to keep going on the path before us.

LOVE THE FACT THAT YOU ARE LOVED

The promise of God's unconditional love for us is the first promise many of us come to know about our relationship with God. The grace of the gospel is shown in the fact that God loved us so much that He sent His Son to be the sacrifice for the debt of His church. Romans 5:8 paints the picture of God's saving love for us: "But God shows his love for us in that while we were still sinners, Christ died for us."

God's love is evident in the fact that He adopted you as His son or daughter. His love is also seen in what He is doing in the lives of believers right now. He is equipping us to love others by His love for us, which is the model and the means by which we love other people. He listens to the pleas and cries of His children. He knows everything that you are going through, and He sympathizes with your daily burdens. He waits for you and even seeks you out in the days you wander from Him. He loves you as His child right now.

God's love is also promised in your days to come. He will not leave you nor forsake you. He is going to finish the work of glory and grace that He began in your life from the moment you trusted Him as your everything. He loves you so much that He looks forward to the day when faith will become sight for you.

> But, as it is written,
> "What no eye has seen, nor ear heard,
>   nor the heart of man imagined,
> what God has prepared for those who love him."
>   (1 Corinthians 2:9)

Jesus is preparing a place for you in glory right at this moment. He is ready and excited to see you face to face when that day comes, but that does not stop Him from loving you right now. Your life is a story arc of the love of God played out in real time. From the beginning of your life to where you are now to eternity to come, God loves you. You cannot remind yourself of His love for you enough. Take time today to remember His unwavering love for you. His love will sustain you in the dark recesses of your waiting.

SEEK HIM IN DESPERATE TIMES

My times of heartache and hurt are the times when God feels most distant—when my prayers feel like they bounce back from my bedroom ceiling. The unrelenting silence and hurt leave me feeling as if He is far away and doesn't want anything to do with me. However, those feelings belie the truth that God is near, sympathetic, and listening.

My circumstances have an ugly way of warping the truth of scriptural promise. My reality paints a picture in my mind of a God who has moved on from me and my future. Yet, God's kindness extends to me in those dark times. He desires to hear my heart, hurt, and cries.

> The LORD is righteous in all his ways
>   and kind in all his works.
> The LORD is near to all who call on him,
>   to all who call on him in truth.
> He fulfills the desire of those who fear him;
>   he also hears their cry and saves them.
>   (Psalm 145:17–19)

There are times when the stresses of life choke out every conceivable bit of goodness that I touch or see. Yet, God is not only present but turns His ear to me in my hard times. He is a shoulder I can cry on even as I question all that I have done and all that is happening around me. All I need to do is go to Him in truth and without any sort of pretense. God desires to hear my hurt, heartache, and doubt.

He desires to hear your cries just as much as the laments that are scattered throughout Scripture, and He will act with saving grace toward those who call out to Him. Do not be wary of God in the midst of your weary days. He is with you and for you as any kind Father would be. Cry out to Him, even when you feel like your prayers have reached their cap, knowing that your Deliverer is near.

HELP YOUR HEART THROUGH MUSIC

Listening to music in our weary days may seem like the least Christian thing on this list, but there is biblical precedent for music being beneficial to the human heart. We see it in the life of King Saul in his last days on the throne. By 1 Samuel 16, a harmful spirit has come upon Saul to torment him. His torment is only eased when music is played for him. So much so that when David played his lyre for the king, Saul was "refreshed and was well, and the harmful spirit departed from him" (1 Samuel 16:23).

This scenario certainly is more descriptive than prescriptive. The Bible is not saying that every time we have a bad day we just need to find the closest lyre player and we will be fine. That is not it at all. What we do see here is that music was used to fight off the darkness in the heart of a man.

There is great power in the truth of God being set to music. That is why the psalms were meant to be sung. These were great anthems meant to express the truth of God and the heart of humanity. Some psalms celebrate the joy of the believer, while other psalms lament the depths and valleys that the believer has to walk through. Both are present in Psalms for the good of people and the glory of God.

James calls for the church in equal measure to cry out to and worship God: "Is anyone among you suffering? Let him pray. Is anyone cheerful? Let him sing praise" (James 5:13). I do not think it is accidental that these words immediately follow the call for the believer to be patient in suffering. Music plays a strong role in the hearts of people and even more so when it is focused toward God.

Find ways to have worshipful music moments beyond the Sunday gathering. Listen to some worship music on your way to work or while you make breakfast. Sing your favorite hymn to yourself. Memorize a psalm to sing in the weariness of the day. Find a way to make music a meaningful part of your daily spiritual life.

FIND A WAY TO FEAST

Your words were found, and I ate them,
and your words became to me a joy
and the delight of my heart,
for I am called by your name,
O Lord, God of hosts.
JEREMIAH 15:16

We spent an entire chapter of this book talking about ways to weave the power of Scripture into our everyday lives. That chapter was filled with a lot of the "what" and "how" of studying Scripture, but it is also vital for us to remember the "why" of studying Scripture, especially on our weariest days.

There are plenty of times in my week where I do not feel like absorbing and studying Scripture during the course of my day. Either my day is too jam-packed or my heart is so depleted that I cannot bring myself to open my Bible and journal. It is the hard line of knowing what I need to do and finding the drive to do it.

To arrive at the place that pushes us to do what we need, we might have to take baby steps. I might not have the drive to sit down for twenty minutes and study Scripture, but I can open up a devotional app on my phone and read for a couple of minutes. I could listen to a section of Scripture read aloud to me through an audio Bible. I may not be mining the depths in my study of Scripture, but it is meaningful sustenance for a weary heart.

There are often long days in our week where we are physically or emotionally worn out, leaving our nerves threadbare. On days like that, the last thing we want to do is to make dinner for our families, but we figure something out. Why? We need it to live.

So it is in our spiritual lives. When the last thing we want to do is to open up our Bible, we need to figure something out. We need time in Scripture to be the spiritual sustenance that keeps us going day after day. Figure out what works for you in terms of getting morsels of Scripture into your life. You may have to start with small bites, but that leads to feasting on the Word that will one day become your greatest joy and delight.

CLING TO WHAT YOU DO NOT SEE

So we do not lose heart. Though our outer self is wasting away, our inner self is being renewed day by day. For this light momentary affliction is preparing for us an eternal weight of glory beyond all comparison, as we look not to the things that are seen but to the things that are unseen. For the things that are seen are transient, but the things that are unseen are eternal.

2 CORINTHIANS 4:16-18

Both our hearts and our eyes can lie to us. They can lead us to believe that things are far worse than they are. When it comes to finding our hope and joy, the enemy will do anything within his power to turn our eyes to what we can see so that we might grasp onto a fleeting moment of hope.

The temptation is to look to our jobs, relationships, possessions, or wealth to give us the glimmer of hope we crave, but all of those things are destined to make us crave more. Those cravings lead to a performance-based trap that we can never get out of on our own. Jesus warns us to find treasures that cannot fade, break, or be stolen: "Do not lay up for yourselves treasures on earth, where moth and rust destroy and where thieves break in and steal, but lay up for yourselves treasures in heaven, where neither moth nor rust destroys and where thieves do not break in and steal. For where your treasure is, there your heart will be also" (Matthew 6:19–21).

I struggle with the warning Jesus offers here because my earthly treasure does not take the shape of a physical possession. I value the words of other people. I care deeply about what people think and say about me. This stems from my childhood and my deep desire of wanting people to look past my disability to see and affirm something meaningful beyond my exterior. That longing has crept its way through my whole life, and it is always crouching in the weeds of my heart.

My flesh wants the praise and words of others to help establish my heart, but there are so many times when the words of others harm my sense of worth and hope. However, God has given me something better than the fickle words of people to fuel me for the long road that stretches in front of me. He has given me a treasure that can never be stolen, damaged, or dimmed, and He planted this treasure in the middle of my broken heart that He continues to mend. He placed the treasure of Himself in our hearts so that we know that both our hope and power do not come from ourselves (2 Corinthians 4:7).

Our hope and joy does not fade when waves of affliction crash over us. What hope we have cannot be robbed by the ways of the world. Our hope is seen as we cast our eyes to a God whose promised love is a fixture in our lives from day to day. We turn our attention to a salvation that is sealed by the very Holy Spirit who dwells with us until the coming of Christ. We put our hope in a Savior who has promised a second advent to rescue His bride the church.

We may have to wait, but we know where to look for hope.

THE SUFFERING SERVANT SHOWS US A PATH FORWARD

The beauty of the life and death of Christ is that He gave us our hope through His work on the cross. The crucifixion of Jesus gave humanity a reason to be hopeful in the face of a hopeless and broken world. On that day at Golgotha, Jesus fulfilled the promised role of "snake crusher" that the Father prophesied in Genesis. Jesus's death made a way for His church to live, but His death also paved the way for the church to suffer.

Jesus has given us a hope to cling to when we have to run the race of faith alone and in the dark. Jesus has also given us a model to look to when we do not know how to take another step. He is the living example of how one can stare down something as foreboding as the cross and yet still pray, "Not my will, but yours, be done," as He pleads with the Father at Gethsemane. The pain as we live is beyond just a threat; it is a calling.

> For to this you have been called, because Christ also suffered for you, leaving you an example, so that you might follow in his steps. He committed no sin, neither was deceit found in his mouth. When he was reviled,

he did not revile in return; when he suffered, he did not threaten, but continued entrusting himself to him who judges justly. He himself bore our sins in his body on the tree, that we might die to sin and live to righteousness. By his wounds you have been healed. For you were straying like sheep, but have now returned to the Shepherd and Overseer of your souls. (1 Peter 2:21–25)

He suffered for you so you could follow Him. He died so that you could live. He went to that tree so that you could be dead to sin but alive to the righteousness He has won you. He embraced the sacrificial call because He knew what His spilled blood would mean for a broken and wayward world. He embraced the will of God because He set His eyes on the joy before Him and the will of the Father.

Jesus is the example of living in endurance with the long run in full view. He knew why He took on flesh and He knew what would follow His prayer in the garden of Gethsemane. Jesus blazed a trail for His church to follow. In the face of overwhelming circumstances, cast your eyes over the horizon and fix your heart on the One who made you and sent you out. Trust the One who sent His Son so that you could live.

LOOK TO THE CLOUD

Jesus is our ultimate example of what a life looks like when it is fully entrusted to the will of the Father. As Hebrews reminds us, Jesus is the greater and better version of any hero from the Old or New Testaments. God in His kindness has given us an example in Christ of how to live out our lives, but He did not stop with Christ. Hebrews also reminds us that those men and women who have gone before us have aspects of their lives worth emulating:

> Therefore, since we are surrounded by so great a cloud
> of witnesses, let us also lay aside every weight, and
> sin which clings so closely, and let us run with endur-
> ance the race that is set before us, looking to Jesus, the
> founder and perfecter of our faith, who for the joy that
> was set before him endured the cross, despising the
> shame, and is seated at the right hand of the throne of
> God. (Hebrews 12:1–2)

The great cloud of witnesses is a reference to many of the Old
Testament people of faith that God used through the centu-
ries. Hebrews 11 lists out the great heroes of faith: Abel, Enoch,
Abraham, Noah, Moses, David, Joseph, Rahab, and many
others.

These are men and women who lived lives of faith. They
did not live perfect lives by any stretch of the imagination. Each
of these people had spectacular failures and damaging sins at
points along their way, but their journeys are not summed up
by their failures. Each person's journey is described as one of
faith that spanned the course of his or her life. They all laid
aside every excuse that came their way, and they ran the race
of faith that stretched out before them.

They looked to the promise of the Savior, knowing that a
faithful God would provide the Messiah He had promised. That
act of faith was credited to them as righteousness. It is that act
of faith that we as the church are supposed to emulate. As they
followed God and waited faithfully for the Christ, so we are
to follow their example as we press forward with endurance.

CONCLUSION

The lifelong race of faith is going on around us whether we like it or not. We have a choice to make: sit on our hands and run aground, run away from our problems, and build a life on unstable ground; or chart a course built firmly on an unshakable hope. The choice is truly ours, but there is only one path to take in view of eternity.

We must trust God with every minute, every day, and every year. We cannot always control what goes on around us, but we can control how we respond. We can choose how we learn from the touchstone moments of our lives and how we can be better prepared for them in the days to come.

My life is not the sum of my most recent successes or failures. My life is grounded in the fact that the God of the universe loves me, is with me, and desires to use me in His grand plan of restoring the created order unto Himself.

That plan is something I get to pursue every day of my life through all the ebbs and flows. It is a plan I can be a part of by trusting God as my everything. As I trust Him with the whole of my life, I live for Him in all the corners of my life.

It is my prayer that this book has not saddled you with a laundry list of things that you must do for the Lord. I pray that this has been an encouragement to love God more and to live for Him in all aspects of your life. Bask in the knowledge that God has chosen you and is now sending you out to tell of His great love for the world.

My prayer for you, believer, is the prayer that Paul prayed over the church at Philippi:

> I thank my God in all my remembrance of you, always in every prayer of mine for you all making my prayer with joy, because of your partnership in the gospel from the first day until now. And I am sure of this, that he who began a good work in you will bring it to completion at the day of Jesus Christ. It is right for me to feel this way about you all, because I hold you in my heart, for you are all partakers with me of grace, both in my imprisonment and in the defense and confirmation of the gospel. For God is my witness, how I yearn for you all with the affection of Christ Jesus. And it is my prayer that your love may abound more and more, with knowledge and all discernment, so that you may approve what is excellent, and so be pure and blameless for the day of Christ, filled with the fruit of righteousness that comes through Jesus Christ, to the glory and praise of God. (Philippians 1:3–11)

May that always be true of us—that we pursued Him until our very last breath. We chased, we fought, we loved, and we trusted. Until Jesus calls us home, let us endure in faith, with all that we are in view of all that He is.

ENDNOTES

1. Dietrich Bonhoeffer, *The Cost of Discipleship* (New York: Touchstone Publishing, 1995), 45.
2. A. J. Broomhall, *Hudson Taylor and China's Open Century, Book Four: Survivors' Pact* (London: Hodder & Stoughton and Overseas Missionary Fellowship, 1984), 154.
3. Christian Literature Society for China, *The China Mission Year Book* (Shanghai: Christian Literature Society for China, 1911), PDF, 281–82.
4. Anna North, "The controversy around Virginia's new abortion bill, explained," February 1, 2019, https://www.vox.com/2019/2/1/18205428/virginia-abortion-bill-kathy-tran-ralph-northam.
5. Paul Strand, "'More Than One-Third of Humanity Will Never Hear About Jesus': Day to Reach the Unreached Set for May 20," April 28, 2018, https://www1.cbn.com/cbnnews/cwn/2018/april/more-than-one-third-of-humanity-will-never-hear-about-jesus-day-to-reach-the-unreached-set-for-may-20.
6. J. D. Greear, "Apple, Inc., and the Kind of Criticism that Helps," October 7, 2013, https://jdgreear.com/not-all-praise-or-criticism-is-created-equal/.
7. "Research: Unchurched Americans Will Talk about Faith, Not Interested in Going to Church," Lifeway Research, June 28, 2016, https://lifewayresearch.com/2016/06/28/unchurched-will-talk-about-faith-not-interested-in-going-to-church/.